**Ben Fergusson**'s debut novel, *The Spring of Kasper Meier*, was awarded the Betty Trask Prize and the HWA Debut Crown, and was shortlisted for the Sunday Times Young Writer of the Year Award. *The Other Hoffmann Sister* and *An Honest Man* complete a trilogy of novels set in the same apartment block in Berlin at key moments in the city's twentieth-century history. His short fiction has been published in journals internationally and in 2020 he won the Seán O'Faoláin International Short Story Prize. He also translates from German, winning a 2020 Stephen Spender Prize for poetry in translation. Ben lives in Berlin with his husband and son.

# TALES FROM THE FATHERLAND

## Two Dads, One Adoption and the Meaning of Parenthood

## Ben Fergusson

abacus
books

ABACUS

First published in Great Britain in 2022 by Little, Brown
This paperback edition published in 2023 by Abacus

1 3 5 7 9 10 8 6 4 2

A CIP catalogue record for this book
is available from the British Library.

ISBN: 978-0-3491-4476-4

Typeset in Caslon by M Rules
Printed and bound in Great Britain by Clays Ltd, Elcograf S.p.A.

Papers used by Abacus are from well-managed forests
and other responsible sources.

Abacus
An imprint of
Little, Brown Book Group
Carmelite House
50 Victoria Embankment
London EC4Y 0DZ

An Hachette UK Company
www.hachette.co.uk

www.littlebrown.co.uk

# Contents

*For Theo, of course,*
*and in memory of Matt Pelly*

*This is a book about being one of two dads. It's a book about the things I have felt and thought about becoming a dad, about being a gay dad, and about being a dad to our son, whom we adopted. Our son has a story too and, in many ways, it is much more interesting than my story. But it isn't my story; it's his. And because it's his story to tell, there are other far more moving, far more important and far more fascinating experiences that we have had as parents that I have left out of this book. And that's fine.*

*I also talk about the experience of adoption. To protect the people involved in that confidential process I have swapped around details, locations, ages and contexts, and changed names. So while the things said here are all true, the people who said them are amalgamations and do not represent specific people. It is an imperfect but necessary way of dealing with a complex and very emotional reality. Which is a perfect way of describing adoption as a whole, not to mention parenthood.*

# 1

# Arrival

## The Call

My childhood fantasy, whenever there was an unexpected knock at the door, was that Charles and Diana had had a breakdown on the A road that ran outside our house and needed a bed for the night. Subsequently, I was always mortified when the door opened on a grinning friend of my parents or some pre-GPS driver lost in the black Oxfordshire countryside.

This huge disparity between reality and the grandiose expectations that I was able to conjure up in milliseconds has never left me. However wonderful a gift, however exciting the content of a letter, however remarkable a phone call, it never quite lives up to the explosion of anticipation I feel when I don't recognise the handwriting on an envelope or the number of an incoming call on my mobile phone. In those seconds before revelation, I imagine boundless riches; I imagine stiff invitations from the Palace, a voice saying, 'Mr Fergusson? I'm connecting you with the Prime Minister.' And so I can't help always being a little disappointed, even when it's something genuinely thrilling.

The call that Wednesday afternoon was a rare exception. I had just finished teaching my weekly English class at the University of Potsdam and saw a missed call on my phone with a Berlin number. I am always waiting for *the* call, the one that is going to change my life, so it's impossible for me to ignore an unidentified number. I always phone back. And then have to pretend to be delighted to have got hold of the bike shop or the bank.

'Frau Schw[mumble],' the voice said.

I sat back in the scratched plastic chair, my fingers still smooth with chalk. It was very promising. Someone official. I had applied for a creative writing grant six months earlier and thought, Of course they call to congratulate you personally, to tell you they've decided to consolidate all the grants into a single grant to reward the most astonishing application they'd ever received.

'It's Ben Fergusson. I had a missed call from this number.'

'Sorry, I missed the name.'

'Ben Fergusson.'

A pause. 'Ah, Herr Fergusson. It's Frau Schwenk.' Our social worker, I now understood. 'Thank you for getting back to me. I'm calling because we have a little boy, four weeks old, who needs a family.'

A woman in our adoption preparation classes had told us she saw stars when she got the call. For me it was more like pressing the pause button on an old VHS. Everything stopped, went silent, juddered a little. I started taking notes in red pen on the back of a vocabulary card, the scratching ballpoint loud in my ears. 'Boy', I scribbled. '4 weeks old'. But that was the sum of the information she could give me over the phone.

'You will need to come to the Senate this evening or tomorrow first thing.' In Berlin, it is rather grandly an office of the State Senate that organises adoptions. 'Then, assuming you are fine with the details, you'll need to meet him tomorrow afternoon. And then if that goes well, you'll need to be ready to bring him home on Friday morning.' A day and a half to prepare for the rest of our lives.

I knew that my husband, Tom, was at his psychotherapy practice until six. I left him a shaky voice message in the empty classroom bright with fluorescent light. I wasn't quite in tears, because I wasn't yet sure it was going to work out. Our social workers had made it clear that we needed to be open-minded when we met our prospective child, in case we didn't bond. Our first social worker, a tough-talking Berliner called Frau Welke, had offered us the slightly perplexing example of a couple she had looked after who rejected a baby, already in their arms at the hospital, because it was called Frieda. Apparently the mother knew a Frieda she hated.

Egbert? Vlad? Turbo? Try as we might, Tom and I couldn't think of a name that we would have found so traumatically awful that we would reject an otherwise perfect baby.

I bumped into my colleague Sowun as I was leaving the office and she asked me which train I was getting.

'The five o'clock,' I said.

'Great. Wait for me. I'll come with you.'

I hadn't spoken to Tom yet. I couldn't tell Sowun before I told Tom, so she chatted to me about her upcoming trip back home to Seoul, landing on the day when all South Korean students take their A Levels at precisely the same time. Behind her, the sun was setting through the window. I squinted and nodded moronically, trying to listen to what she was saying, but feeling that she was very far away behind a sheet of glass.

Back home, pinching my bottom lip at the kitchen table, an undrunk cup of tea at my elbow, I watched the grey ticks of my WhatsApp voice message to Tom turn blue. A few seconds later he called back, desperate for details.

'How old is he?'

'Four weeks.'

'Where is he now?'

'I don't know. They'll tell us tomorrow, I think.'

'Is he well?'

'She said a healthy baby.'

I could hear the cracking of the floorboards in his office as he shifted his weight.

'Maybe this is it.'

'Maybe,' I said.

Tom's practice is outside Berlin, and it would be another two hours before he got home. Because we hadn't even met our son yet, I didn't want to call my family and get them excited about something that might not be happening. I tried to read, but found myself staring out into the night sky, the paperback spatchcocked on my chest. I turned on the TV, but anything interesting was too difficult to concentrate on and anything banally entertaining seemed to clash with the moment. So I poured myself a Scotch and played a mindless strategy game on my computer for two hours as the night set in.

After many rounds of hugging, Tom and I went through the schedule for the next few days. We had the first meeting at the Senate from eight to eleven in the morning, and were meeting our potential son from three to six in the afternoon that same day. All going well, we would be picking him up on Friday morning at eleven. This, we worked out, left us a window of four hours on Thursday in which to purchase everything a baby might need for its first night at home, as well as a car seat to get him back from the hospital.

While Tom did a trolley dash around Rossmann, the local

drugstore chain – buying multiple bottles and dummies when he wasn't sure which type was right – I marched into the nearest baby clothing shop and said: 'I need all the clothes for a four-week-old baby boy.'

The friendly but bewildered shop assistant said, 'What size is he?'

I approximated what I thought the size of a four-week-old baby was with my hands. She frowned.

'I mean, how tall is he?'

'I don't know.'

'How much does he weigh?'

'About three kilos when he was born.'

'And now?'

'I don't know.'

'Is this your baby?' she asked.

Once I'd cleared up the confusion, we set about piling up socks, hats, rompers and sleeping bags on the counter, our search punctuated by her suddenly remembering essentials – 'You need hundreds of muslins!' – and offering sage advice – 'Too big is always better than just fits!'

That same weekend I returned to exchange half of what I'd bought because I'd guessed most of the sizes wrong and, in my post-arrival stupor, had boil-washed all the woollens.


## A Brief Historical Interlude

To be clear, we weren't simply incompetently ill prepared for the advent of our first child. The absurd speed of our son's arrival and our planned unpreparedness, like so much of German public life, is intricately interwoven with the country's twentieth-century history.

I was really disturbed during the Brexit debate to read

accusations of Germany using the EU as a tool for some sort of Nazi-style power grab to create a unified Europe under its Machiavellian control.[1] It is impossible to overemphasise the extent to which, over seventy-five years after the war ended, the whole of Germany's civil apparatus continues to be geared towards eliminating the ills of the Nazi era. Of course, Germany, like every country in Europe, still has problems with political extremes, but every area of public life here, from education and health to Germans' relationship with video surveillance, is deeply influenced by the country's past. And the same is true of adoption.

As part of their bid to build a greater German Reich in Europe, the Nazis weaponised all elements of civil society, and this included the care system. In the mid-1930s the SS set up the *Lebensborn* (literally 'Font of Life') programme, providing welfare to married and unmarried mothers in return for them giving birth to their Aryan children in SS adoption homes. These children, some 20,000 by the end of the war, were then syphoned off to party members who couldn't have children naturally.

More terrifying still was the role of adoption in the *Generalplan Ost*, the Nazis' scheme to annex and racially purify huge swathes of Eastern Europe for Hitler's much-vaunted *Lebensraum* ('living space'). Focused on Poland, the Nazis systematically kidnapped up to 400,000 children that they considered to be of German descent and thus Aryan-Nordic. Only 15 to 20 per cent of these children were ever returned to their biological parents and many thousands died being transported or were murdered in concentration camps when no homes were found for them.

In the light of these horrors, West Germany set about embedding the right of parents to their children in the *Grundgesetz*, the country's post-war democratic constitution. As a result, judges in modern-day Germany are still deeply wary of legally removing children from their biological parents. There are still, sadly, many cases in which children can't be left in the homes into which they were born but, in Germany, children removed by the court are generally not put up for adoption. Instead, Germany has a three-tier care programme, consisting of adoption, short-term foster care and then a middle way called long-term foster care, where the majority of children land who will never be able to live with their biological families again.

This all means that children in Germany who are adopted are nearly always children who for countless reasons have not been removed by the court, but have consciously been put up for adoption by one or more of their parents, nearly always their mother. Generally mothers make this decision before or just after the child is born and they often don't tell the authorities about their pregnancy until they've gone into labour, or sometimes in the hours or days after birth. Sometimes the children have been abandoned, often in hospitals, and sometimes they have been placed in one of the country's *Babyklappen*, literally 'baby flaps', where mothers are allowed to leave their children anonymously without risk of being prosecuted for abandonment. The latter system is designed to reduce the number of children who die each year after being abandoned in unsafe locations, though its effectiveness is contentious.

The consequence of this set-up is that, unlike most other countries, the majority of adoptions in Germany involve babies. It also means that there are relatively few children who are put up for adoption in the first place, because children over two almost always end up in foster care. In Berlin, which is both a city and a federal state with a population of about 4 million, around eighty children are adopted per year by parents who had no previous relationship to them – that is to say, children who weren't adopted by a relative, like a step-parent. For those eighty children, the main adoption organisation, the Berlin Senate Office for Education, Young People and Families, has around two thousand prospective adopters on its books.

This comes of course with advantages for children in need of adoption. For a start, they are more or less guaranteed adoptive parents, and social workers have much more choice when it comes to picking exactly the right parents to fulfil a child's specific needs. People often talk about adoptive parents being on the waiting list for a child, but there is in fact no waiting list. Instead, the authorities refer to 'a pool' of approved prospective adopters, who are carefully matched with children by the social workers in the Senate Office.

We were incredibly lucky – the gap between approval and our son's arrival was just three months. The average is one to two years. The hard truth, though, banged into us throughout the whole year-long process, is that being approved for adoption does not mean you will ever be offered a child.

## The Meeting House

Before our son arrived, Tom and I often talked about how our social worker could possibly decide whether or not we matched a child that was potentially only a few weeks old. And yet, from the day we brought him home, we have been astounded by how perfectly matched he is. Perhaps, blinded by love, we would say this about any child we adopted. But whenever we meet up with other adoptive parents, I look at their children and I look at Theo and I think, It could only have been him.

I was very moved recently by someone captioning a picture of their biological daughter with the line 'I'm so glad it was you'. A sentiment that captures the unbelievably unlikely series of cosmic machinations that led to her having *this* child rather than the billions of other possible children that might have been created by her ovaries and her partner's sperm if they'd made love a second earlier or later. But I have been surprised that my gut feeling when I watch my son thudding off through the flat to fetch another book is 'Of course it was you'. I am shocked by how inevitable he seems to me, how completely familiar.

We met him in the doorway of a building in Mariendorf, a quarter of Berlin famous for its immigration centre. It has been the first port of call for the millions of refugees who fled first Eastern Europe, then East Germany and, more recently, Southern Europe, the Middle East and North Africa – all also in search of refuge, looking for a new home.

Both we and the nurse who had looked after him for the first few weeks of his life arrived too early and the building was locked. We said hello, my heart pounding in my throat at the sight of the car seat with a muslin pegged over the top.

'Could we see him?' Tom said.

I was worried this might not be allowed, somehow. But I also didn't want to stand making small talk, pretending that our prospective son was not a few inches from the ends of our toes.

'Of course,' she said.

We knelt, she lifted the muslin, and we peered in. He was asleep, tiny beneath the folds of his colourful hat and knitted cardigan, his little face waxy and doll-like.

The social worker arrived on time and we were shown into a large room with a big table, upon which the nurse set Theo's car seat. She chattered on about his routine, how much he ate, how much she had enjoyed looking after him during those few weeks. I took down notes on my mobile phone, intermittently looking up at him. 'Who *are* you?' I wanted to ask him, but he was perfectly still, his tight lips and tight lids inscrutable.

Then he stirred, blinked and woke up.

His eyes were black, and the nurse asked us if we wanted to hold him. He started crying the moment he was in my arms. I joggled him around the room but he was inconsolable, his face becoming all mouth and reddening to a rich crimson as the nurse shouted out instructions like a shepherd to a collie. 'Lift him up.' 'Hold the dummy in.' 'Talk to him.' 'Sway! Sway!' Eventually, after ten minutes that felt like thirty, he quietened.

The nurse made up his milk. I sat down and the social worker packed a pillow around me that resembled a giant fluorescent snake. They tucked Theo into the crook of my arm and gave me the tiny bottle. That was the moment. Tom asked the nurse and the social worker some questions, I listened and nodded, and got lost in his face, his hesitant drinking, the perfection of his fingernails and his creased little palms.

'So,' the social worker said. 'We're going to leave the room now and you can have a think about whether it fits.'

We waited for them to leave and, when we thought they were out of earshot, we looked at each other and said, 'Well, yes of course, no?'

'Of course.'

I felt as if the momentousness of the decision required more time, more discussion, but what else was there to say?

Then we had half an hour just to sit with him asleep in our arms, impossibly small, radiating an impossible amount of heat.

## The Pick-up

A car seat and a blanket: the only two items required to be in your possession if you want to take a baby home from a hospital in Berlin. Whether or not you actually have a car is immaterial. So the next day, a cool autumn morning at the end of October, we set out on foot with a mustard-coloured blanket folded up in our new; empty car seat. The pavement and the streets were strewn with lemon-yellow leaves. Yellow buses splashed through black puddles and the high song of the S-Bahn train filled the indigo sky.

I thought about the impossibility of fathoming great change. When we had moved back to Berlin from London three years earlier, people had asked me, 'How do you feel about the move?', said, 'This time tomorrow you'll be living in Berlin.' And I replied with some version of 'I know, we're so excited', but really I couldn't comprehend it. It was completely cognitive. I understood it would be happening, but I didn't believe it. I understood too that we were going to pick up our son, but how could I possibly believe that two hours later we would be at home with our baby?

I was reminded of my sister's planned Caesarean; how odd it was to speak to her from the hospital at three o'clock, her telling me to think about her at four o'clock when my niece would be alive in the world.

We too were beginning our family at an institutionally allotted time – 11 a.m. on a Friday morning. Life is filled with change, but there are only a few moments in which we are aware that we are standing in one life and that imminently we will be standing in another. Alice before the looking glass.

We met up with Theo and the nurse for the second time in a room on the second floor of the heart clinic of a large hospital. It was a family room that had been converted from a ward, the strips of lights and plugs for the hospital machinery still circling the wall high up, like a picture rail. We chatted about the nurse's last night with him and how much she and her family would miss him. He started crying; we both looked at him.

'Should I pick him up?'

'He's your son,' she said, smiling, but looked a little heart-broken as I lifted him into my arms.

Because the first stages of the adoption process require you to remain as anonymous as possible you are told to avoid using your name, even when talking to officials at the hospital. Instead of showing your passport, the Senate gives you a stamped piece of paper that states 'The bearer of this letter may collect [name of child] from [name of hospital]'. It was necessarily the only way we were required to identify ourselves when we thanked the nurse and put Theo in his pristine car seat. But it seemed so inconsequential, that piece of paper; too flimsy, too colourless for its mammoth import.

Our friend Konstanze picked us up and drove us back through Berlin, showering our sleeping baby with compliments. She stayed for a coffee while I ran out and picked up a few last things we had forgotten to buy in our four-hour rush the day before.

It was then, Tom later told me, that he knew. Konstanze had left, I was still trying to fathom what baby-bumpers were and whether he needed them, and Tom leaned over Theo on the bed and locked eyes with him. Tom was overcome with a feeling that everything was going to be all right and he heard himself making a silent promise that he was going to look after him for ever.

That night, once Theo fell asleep, we placed him in his Baby Bay – a kind of wooden cot that clips onto the side of your mattress – and climbed into bed. We had barely slept the night before in anticipation and now, exhausted, we lay sleepless again.

I didn't know that babies breathe quite erratically in the first few months and I was terrified that he was going to just stop. I tracked each breath in the semi-darkness, willing along the next. There was a terrible tension between my desire to sleep and my sense that I needed to remain completely vigilant. As I tried to drift off and tried to focus on our son I began to feel deeply anxious. A loud thought kept intruding, telling me – for some unknown reason – that his name was actually Jonathan, the name of a friend's nephew, and I was too exhausted to shift my focus. Of course, I thought, lying there, I'm going to go crazy. Right now. I'm having a psychotic breakdown and I'm going to have to run out into the street screaming.

I didn't have a psychotic breakdown. I drifted off in the end, but never really fell asleep. The next day Tom told me that he had also had frightening, crazed thoughts as he lay in bed, and this was a consolation. It's the last detailed memory I have of the first days of our adoption.

## Life in the Aquarium

What I recall of the first few months after our son arrived is constant amber twilight. As autumn moved into winter, the days darkened and shortened and we adapted to our son's four-hour rhythm. He did not yet differentiate day and night and so it lost meaning for us too. He woke desperately hungry and screaming, ate, and then fell asleep again. The only change to this schedule was about 4.30 in the afternoon when he would begin to cry uncontrollably and could only be soothed by being wedged under one of our stubbled chins and rocked for an hour.

At night we kept a lamp on in the living room so that we could move about in the semi-darkness. Berlin's short winter days and steel-grey skies required the lamp to be left on almost constantly, dim and orange, like the Centennial Light that has been burning for over a century in the Livermore-Pleasanton Fire Department. We discovered that Theo was soothed by white noise, particularly recordings of rain and waves, and, as we stumbled out of bed for another bottle, I often felt like we were living underwater, the air the gaslight brown of David Fincher films.

After eating, Theo would sleep for an hour in his cot or his day bed. During the day, this hour presaged a brief period of intense activity as we washed clothes, fed ourselves, showered and called relatives and friends. He would wake crying and would only go back to sleep if he was lying on top of one of us, trapping us beneath him for the subsequent three hours before his next feed.

I discovered that every day for five hours there was a seemingly endless documentary series on an obscure German TV channel that told the natural history of the coast of the USA through drone footage and dubbed interviews with lobster catchers, fishermen and marine biologists. Flying over the Florida mangroves, the rocky coast of Maine, the beaches of the Hamptons, one unchallenging episode would bleed into the next and, before I knew it, it was time for another feed and I'd realise I'd forgotten to eat.

It was an overwhelming time, but also, as the cold hardened outside, an incredibly cosy one. Although no one in their right mind would suggest that children are a good remedy for anxiety, I did find a huge amount of comfort in the immediacy of my son's needs and the clarity of my task. If I abandoned him, he would die. If I didn't feed him, he would die. If I didn't change and clean him, he would become sick and die.

Since puberty, my feeling as I climb into bed has always been one of failure. It's an anxiety that sits high in my stomach, a feeling that there's so much that I might have achieved if I hadn't squandered my time. It is this anxiety that my son – for the time being – has cured me of. In part, the change has been physical. I used to lie in the dark pondering my failures, but these days I get my head on the pillow and collapse into sleep.

More importantly, though, a day with Theo is a day in which I am – for better or worse – very present. Childcare requires you to form a radically new relationship with time, existing where once you planned and worried. Problems and anxieties are constant companions, but also require an enforced Buddhistic acceptance. The terrible things that could happen to your child are so exponentially vast that your only option most of the time is to consciously stop yourself from thinking about them and let them drift away again.

Boredom too must be tackled with radical acceptance. I sometimes kicked against it, thought: How am I possibly going to get through the next hour until Tom comes home? But you have no choice. You move through the hour with primordial slowness, understanding but not really believing that at some unfathomably distant point in the future you will talk to an adult again, you will bathe, you will sleep.

## Sleep and Madness

Beyond these flickers of grace, parenthood, particularly early parenthood, is a huge challenge mentally. The crucible of most of these issues is sleep. It is not just that you don't get much sleep, it's that the sleep you do get is also not very good sleep.

Even now when Theo sleeps through the night in his own room, I wake up numerous times listening for the crackle of the baby phone. We have always alternated night shifts and whoever is on gets what we refer to as 'a lie-in', which means getting to sleep until 7.30 a.m. (8.30 a.m. at the weekend). But the person who wasn't 'on' will also have woken up every time Theo cried and is not much better rested than the night-shift worker when they crawl out of bed at 7 a.m. on a good day, 5 a.m. on a bad.

Real sleep deprivation is powerfully different from what I'd previously understood as exhaustion. There is a sort of feverish alertness to it, what Jean Rhys describes as when 'everything is like a dream and you are starting to know what things are like underneath what people say they are'.[2]

You experience subtle personality changes. I became more short-tempered; not just annoyed by Tom, but furious about the myriad tiny things he'd done, while remaining convinced that my lack of sleep had nothing to do with my gruffness. I felt as if my skin had been flayed, that I was raw and unable to protect myself from attack.

About eight months after our son arrived, I read Emma Jane Unsworth's account of her struggle with postnatal depression after the birth of her first child.[3] In it she recounts how she felt during the first months and years after her son was born, deeply sleep-deprived, broken, and guilty that she felt so broken:

> My mind has been darkening steadily since December, a month or so after the baby was born. I have accumulated layer upon layer of bad feeling; of negativity, rage and doom. I am swollen with it, waiting to explode. 'I think you have postnatal depression,' The Cartoonist [her partner] says regularly. 'I think you should go and talk to someone. A therapist. Your GP.'

If I'd read the article a year earlier, I'd have thought, How difficult – but what a caring partner, encouraging her to find help. But reading it after a tough night with our then eight-month-old, I thought, Of course she's depressed, you twat. Save your fucking advice and start pulling your weight. I may have been projecting a little.

Having shared those early months fifty-fifty and still been at times raging, exhausted and out of my mind, I felt – and still feel – that postnatal depression, if not inevitable, is certainly a pretty comprehensible reaction to the realities of early child-care, especially if you're taking most of them on by yourself.

In those first six months, Tom and I would lie on our sofa and ritualistically repeat: imagine doing this alone having just given birth. Imagine doing this throbbing with hormones. Imagine doing this after our bellies had swollen up over the last nine months and we had pushed a baby out of our genitals, which were now wrecked and bleeding, and we couldn't go to the loo, because of our haemorrhoids.

And what about Caesareans? Imagine a scenario in which you have just had major abdominal surgery and, as the anaes-thetic funk begins to clear, someone hands you a baby. I was knackered and Tom was knackered, we forgot sentences we had begun, we were regularly startled out of gormless day-dreams in the middle of rooms, we napped on chairs and sofas, on the floor. But when my sister got home from hospital after her Caesarean she couldn't even get up the stairs to her bed or sit up to breastfeed. And two weeks after that her husband went back to work.

Why are we surprised that so many women struggle mentally and emotionally after experiencing such profound physical changes, often including extreme physical pain, and then being left to care for a tiny life more or less alone? The answer, of course, is that we are surprised because we don't actually consider what they have experienced as extreme.

My mum once had a chat with a surgeon she knew about her experiences of major surgery and he said, 'What major surgery did *you* have?'

'Three Caesareans,' she said.

'Oh,' said the surgeon, 'that's obstetrics. That doesn't count.'

My and Tom's interactions with medical professionals were brief and reassuring. We had to find a midwife at short notice.

She told us which powdered milk to buy, showed us how to feed our baby and bathe him, watched over us as we changed his nappies, told us which baby cream was acceptable and which we should actually buy. Her presence was completely reassuring and the main tenet of her advice was 'You're doing much better than you think you are'.

I had steeled myself for a battle. Most of my female friends and family members had had deeply ambivalent experiences with doctors, midwives and health visitors when they gave birth. They were often made to feel that there was a right way to have a baby – naturally, without pain relief, followed by years of abundant breastfeeding – and that they were systematically failing.

They would spend hours in labour being told they had come to hospital too early, then be told when they returned that they were too far along for an epidural. They would not produce milk, not produce enough milk, have to feed their babies on bleeding nipples, their breasts solid and excruciatingly painful with mastitis. Their babies would lose weight, they would feel like exhausted failures, and the message would keep coming back: you need to try harder, you have to persevere.

I'm not saying that this is the experience of all women or even most women when they have children. In my experience, people who have a terrible time giving birth and breastfeeding talk about it, and people who have a good experience don't; they have a child to look after and their relatively smooth birthing experience is comparatively less interesting than their newborn. But what I do think is true is that, as adopters who are both men, we have experienced nothing that comes close to the trauma many mothers experience in the first months of parenthood when they are physically and mentally at their limits and are being treated as if there's nothing wrong.

Time and again my and Tom's anxieties are soothed by the

lack of expectations we face. Our doctor outlines any treatments and vaccinations Theo's due and doesn't comment on our final decision. Our social workers were interested in our thoughts about when Theo should go to nursery, but didn't pressure us either way. People respond thoughtfully when we talk about whether or not we should have a second child, but don't make us feel that there's a right decision to be made.

The differences in our experiences as new parents compared to those of our female friends and family members don't end there. But these reflections were made in the confines of our flat. The reality of how starkly our experience of parenting differed from that of the straight families we knew only became viscerally apparent when we packed our son into his blue felt winter suit and gingerly ventured out onto the streets of Berlin.

# Fathoming a Family

## Good Sex

I worked out I was gay in 1993 during an episode of *The Good Sex Guide* on Channel 4\* presented by a platinum-blonde Margi Clarke. I watched the half-hour show – daringly brash then, incredibly tame by today's standards† – on the small white Sony television in my bedroom, bending the looped aerial on top to try and free the soft-core nudity from its snowy static.

I was thirteen, and for exactly a week I had been masturbating. For seven days I imagined making love to the blonde woman in the varsity cardigan whom I'd seen in a copy of *Mayfair*. Someone at school had stolen it for me from their dad's stack in return for three battered pound coins saved from my lunch money. Now I was confronted with moving legs and breasts. And then the camera cut to a team of male footballers showering.

It wasn't until I was in my twenties that I realised that, for many people, this process of self-discovery is gradual, often

---

\* My sole source of information about queerness throughout the 1990s.

† They just showed the first male erection on British television.

tentative, taking months, years, sometimes even decades to form into something concrete. But I knew immediately. It didn't feel like a revelation, in the sense that I wasn't overcome with a wave of self-perception that explained years of tell-tale signs (though there had been tell-tale signs). I just thought, Oh, I'm gay. I'd better not tell anybody until I go to university.

Thus I entered what Eve Sedgwick described as 'that long Babylonian exile known as queer childhood'.[1] University was five years away, and in fact I wouldn't tell anyone for another seven years. It was a long time to keep a secret. But then again the notion of telling anyone while I was still at school was so absurd that I didn't even stop to think about it.

In some ways 1993 was a great time to realise you were gay in rural south Oxfordshire. Times had moved on enough that I had actually met someone who was openly gay – an actor who directed a play at the open-air theatre in our village – and I had witnessed his sexuality being viewed, at worst, as something rather exotic and urbane by my parents and their friends. When my siblings and I included being gay in our long list of hypothetical things we might do that would upset our parents – joining the army and becoming zealously religious were the two no-nos – they were vocally nonplussed about any of us turning out to be queer.

My sexual awakening occurred just before the explosion of the internet. Thus I avoided having to make sense of my yearnings through online pornography, avoided having to pick my way through an endless carousel of hung, hairless men finding creative ways to penetrate each other. Instead, I got my kicks looking at treasure trails in the underpants and swimwear section of the Littlewoods catalogue and pretending to browse for posters at the Athena store in Oxford so that I could catch a glimpse of Kevin Costner with one nipple out.

In other ways, of course, it was a terrible time to be gay. At my all-boys state comprehensive school in Didcot, being a swot already meant that I was called 'gay' on a daily basis. So liberally were slurs like 'poof' and 'bender' thrown around – a 'faggot' was still a meatball in 1990s south Oxfordshire, a 'fag' still a cigarette – that straight students were the victims of homophobic bullying far more often than those of us who actually turned out to be queer. But, of course, those of us who turned out to be queer also heard every day that we embodied something so terrible that our very being was the lowest insult you could fling at someone. What was worse than being a poof?

My gran's proposed solution to bullying was the age-old classic: 'Sticks and stones may break my bones but words will never hurt me.' There were a lot of sticks and stones, though. The general suspicion that I was gay meant that I was punched regularly. One boy liked to throw actual stones at me if he saw me outside school.* A group of boys in the year below – their being younger added to my shame – egged me while I was walking to class.† I was regularly shoved into walls, spat at, tripped and hit.

As extreme as it might sound, I had a very real sense that admitting I was gay would mean that someone might actually kill me. They sometimes whispered it into my ear as they punched me: 'I'm going to kill you, Fergie.' Fergie was my nickname at school – like the princess. And of course Thatcher's Section 28 was still in place in the UK, so if I had come out to any of my teachers and told them I was being bullied it would've been illegal for them to tell me that there

---

* This boy was recently chatting to my sister about what a fun guy I'd been at school. He had tormented me for two years. I was literally terrified of him and he couldn't even honour that torment by recalling it.
† Brown suede. My first proper jacket. Ruined. My mum took it to the dry cleaner's but it was unsaveable.

was actually nothing wrong with me. That I didn't deserve to be bullied.

I paint this picture not to elicit sympathy per se, but to illustrate how baffled I was when, in 2006, a few years after I'd come out, I met my future husband and he told me on the morning after the night before that he wanted to adopt.

I didn't know what to say. It wasn't that I didn't want to have children, it was just that I'd never even fathomed that it was a possibility. Adoption for same-sex parents was still illegal in every part of the UK bar England, and in nearly every other country in the world, including Germany where Tom lived. Celebrities, gay or straight, weren't yet having children via surrogates. And, whereas I'd met one gay person before I worked out I was gay, I didn't know a single queer person with a child. I hadn't even heard of one. The only reference to queer parenting I'd even witnessed was a joke in *Friends* that revolved around Chandler and Joey failing to chat up a woman they fancied because she mistook them for gay adoptive parents.

## Do Role Models Matter?

Would I have felt differently if there had been role models in my life? Gay parents on TV, in my school, in ads at the bus stop? I think I can say, yes, definitely. Because I used to be a massive homophobe. And this was only ameliorated through other people's example.

When Tony Blair's Labour government announced their plans to allow civil partnerships and adoption rights for people in same-sex relationships I didn't feel positive about it. There were many queer people who felt, and continue to feel, uncomfortable about gay marriage on the basis that one of the few advantages of being in a marginalised sexual minority is that you don't have to be confined by the conservative strictures so many heterosexual people struggle with. As Fran Lebowitz put it:

> Do you think gay marriage is progress? Are you kidding me? This was one of the good things about being gay. I am stunned that the two greatest desires apparently of people involved in the gay rights movement are gay marriage and gays in the military. Really? To me these are the two most confining institutions on the planet: people used to pretend to be gay to get out of going into the army.[2]

I would like to say that, like Fran Lebowitz, my discomfort with gay marriage and gay adoption was political. And indeed when I talked to people about it at the time I put it in those terms. 'Why do we want to be part of a ceremony that we've been excluded from for the last four millennia? If we keep being told it's not for us, then we should just reject it. We should be pointing out how dumb marriage is rather than trying to co-opt it.'

These are really valid arguments that many bright and engaged queer people took up and continue to take up. They're the kind of morally astute, historically aware arguments that I would like to be able to forcefully make. But the truth is that the idea of men marrying men and having babies – well, it just made me feel weird.

I remember very clearly the first time I heard an American interviewee on Radio 4 refer to his husband after same-sex marriage became legal in Massachusetts in 2004. I felt queasy. I was embarrassed for him, in fact. It sounded put on to me, artificial. I felt like he was doing what gay people are so often accused of doing: he was rubbing my face in it. Why couldn't he just be quietly gay at home and not trouble us all with his wacky ideas about matrimony?

I believed, back then, that internalised homophobia meant absorbing society's hatred of queer people and applying it to yourself, because, deep down, you hated yourself too and you felt that you deserved to be hated by society. I've never liked my voice, always felt it was too 'sissy', and was mortified as a teenager when people mistook me for my mother when I answered the phone. I always felt deeply ashamed about how bad at sports I was and still feel a rush of pit-sweat horror any time a ball rolls off a football pitch or basketball court and some teenager shouts, 'Mate! Can you throw it back?' To this day, I feel embarrassed about being caught listening to pop artists like Madonna or Kylie, who are considered gay icons. And still, when someone says something like, 'Oh I wouldn't have guessed you were gay,' I feel a little thrill that I have passed as straight.

I have always been well aware that all of this is internalised homophobia.

My realisation over the past decade, though, has been how structural homophobia – and thus internalised homophobia – really is. It is not just that I see things in myself that are queer and feel a sense of revulsion, the same sense of revulsion that my bullies at school felt. It is also that my vocabulary about my experience of being a gay man is so limited and my stock of examples about what it means to be queer is so scant that I struggle to have the most basic conversations about my feelings. I find it easy to talk about feelings in the abstract, easy to talk about other people's emotional concerns, but almost impossible to talk about my own emotions with anyone but my husband. My sense is of literally not having the vocabulary to talk about it.

I wasn't fully out to everyone in my family until I was in my mid-twenties, meaning that I just didn't talk about how I really felt for the first post-pubescent decade of my life. Like a lot of gay men, I became a very good listener through this experience. And I became very good at talking with emotion and enthusiasm about any range of cultural and pop-cultural topics that fascinated me. It is, I think, one of the reasons that gay men are so often celebrated as raconteurs. But beneath all that chatter there was an ocean of anxiety stirring in my belly, the waves always threatening to thicken into a squall.

I don't think that this silence was lost on the people who loved me. I remember talking to my friend Jamie about someone I was seeing and he said, 'Like, what kind of relationship do you have with this guy?' I was stumped. 'Friends,' I said, and felt ashamed for saying it. But I literally didn't know how I was meant to talk about gay relationships to my straight friends. At some very deep level too I had learned in school that talking about how I actually felt was dangerous. Literally dangerous – I would have been physically hurt for doing it. To this day, when I talk openly about my emotions I still feel that danger high up in my stomach. I still have that same sense of opening a window and climbing out onto the ledge where the slightest gust of wind, the smallest misstep, is going to pitch me over the edge.

In 2015 the openly gay fashion designer Domenico Dolce (one half of Dolce & Gabbana) caused a small uproar when he told the Italian magazine *Panorama*: 'We oppose gay adoptions. The only family is the traditional one.' He went on to describe children born through IVF, sperm donation and surrogacy as 'children of chemistry, synthetic children. Rented uterus, semen chosen from a catalogue.'[3] Appalling sentiments, unquestionably. Sentiments that he later apologised for. But there was still a little part of me that sympathised with him. Because when I was a kid, men and women had kids. And gay people were creepy.

In the contemporary American Bible Belt, in Hungary and Russia, officials are constantly trying to hide any positive images of homosexuality away from children's eyes, so damaging do they consider a single one. But what about the queer child?

Growing up in a straight society, every queer child experiences their own informal conversion therapy. I was bombarded with images of heterosexual parenting the moment I was able to focus on the 'Mother and Baby' section at the local supermarket. And when I was old enough to start consuming apparently straight, sexless popular culture, I was presented with a cavalcade of mincing Disney villains, from Shere Khan and Scar to Captain Hook and Jafar, whose evil was embodied in the cartoonishly queer performances of the straight male actors voicing them.

When I was old enough to graduate to film as a teenager, and long before I was able to watch anything explicitly queer, I had already met the demented lesbian in Hitchcock's *Rebecca*, the weak, effeminate and morally corrupt homosexual in Mel Gibson's *Braveheart*, the dangerously ambiguous, split-personality bisexual in *Basic Instinct*, and the crazed trans killer in *Silence of the Lambs*.

It is, thus, no great surprise that, in moments of stress and crisis, there will always be a little part of me that thinks I shouldn't be allowed to have a family. The oddest manifestation of this type of internalised homophobia is when I meet another obviously gay man – in a meeting at work, perhaps, at a restaurant or on a plane – and I think, I wonder what it's like to be gay. And a second later remember: Oh yes – I'm gay.

This is driven by internalised homophobia, but it is also driven by a lack of role models. And a lack of role models is not just a problem of absence, it is a problem of diversity.

## Dramatic Diversity

I was lucky enough to grow up at a time when being gay was not illegal. I was lucky enough to grow up at a time when I knew that gay people existed. When I was in my teens and early twenties, gay life was no longer invisible on TV, but the few films and TV shows I had seen about gay people – even the ones I loved – presented a quite narrow vision of what it meant to be a gay man. And it was a vision that did not include two men or two women having children together.

In *Tales of the City*, in *Queer as Folk*, in *Priest*, *Tinsel Town*, *Philadelphia* and *This Life* I understood that gay men were either deeply into 'the scene' or were deeply repressed; that they had sex with men they met in gay clubs or in parks and toilets, where they would likely get 'gay bashed'; that even if they were in a relationship, they would probably still sleep with a lot of other people, and by sleeping with a lot of other people they would catch AIDS.

There is nothing wrong with going to gay clubs, having sex in parks or not being monogamous. It's just that it all takes a lot of guts. Heading out on my own to a gay club? Venturing into the bushes in a park to have sex with someone who might kill me? Taking drugs that might kill me? At twenty, these things terrified me. I just wanted to meet someone nice down the pub and at some point after that start having pleasant sex with them in my flat.

I never questioned these scant representations of what it meant to be a gay man because I had no other picture of how you might do it. As much as I'd like to say that I understood this was drama and it required dramatic things to happen – that there were plenty of gay men passing me on the street every day who had sex with their boyfriends in their flats, who had taken drugs without dying and had had sex outdoors without being hit over the head – I was convinced that everything I'd seen on TV was more or less based on fact. I believed that the problem was with me, that I just had to learn to enjoy these things, like I'd learned to enjoy beer and olives.

I would muse on this on my blow-up sofa in my childhood bedroom, not with terror, but with a sort of sad acceptance. At nineteen, in the light of the lava lamp, I watched *Queer as Folk* on that fuzzy Sony TV, anxiously eating Cool Doritos, thinking, At some point I'm going to have to get up enough courage to go to Soho where some older man is going to take me home, give me drugs and rim me.

I recently read an interview with Parminder Nagra, the star of the 2002 film *Bend It Like Beckham*, which made a star of Keira Knightley. Even if you were Knightley's biggest fan, you would have to admit that Nagra was the star of that film. But being a British-Asian woman, Hollywood did not open its door to her as widely as it did to her co-star. And in those roles Nagra does now land, she is often required to put on an Indian accent, even when it isn't relevant to her character.[4] Two decades after her stereotype-busting role, this actor with Indian heritage is being forced to play a less diverse, more expected version of an Indian woman, and the same remains true for gay characters.

There are the straight men playing gay and they have two approaches to it. There is the school of the late Willie Garson in *Sex and the City* and Eric Stonestreet in *Modern Family*. They play a high-camp version of a stereotypical gay man. Then there is the school of Heath Ledger in *Brokeback Mountain* and Trevante Rhodes in *Moonlight*. They just play the gay man as themselves – a straight man. Then, like Nagra being required to 'play Indian', there are the gay actors who are required to 'play gay'. Zachary Quinto in *American Horror Story: Horror House*, Sean Hayes in *Will & Grace* – playing gay characters who are much more stereotypically gay than they are themselves.

This binary of 'straight-acting gay man' and 'stereotypically gay man' that we see on TV represents, of course, real people. And we need to keep representing them. There are gay figures like Russell Tovey and Pete Buttigieg whom you would read as straight on first meeting them. And there are gay people like Alan Carr and Billy Porter whom you would immediately recognise as gay in all of their beautiful campness. But I still feel that there is a massive swathe of gay men – the biggest swathe, I would argue – who are somewhere in the middle.

I would include myself in that swathe. No one is surprised I'm gay. Some people think I'm gay when they meet me, some people think I'm straight. It is a grey area that a lot of us exist in. I see this man, and thus myself, reflected in Zachary Quinto and Sean Hayes when I see them being interviewed, but not in the queer characters they play on TV. In fact, twenty-two years after *Queer as Folk*, what I still almost never see is any reflection of a gay man like myself on TV. Jonathan Groff in *Looking* captures it. Ncuti Gatwa in *Sex Education* captures it. But it is rare. And as James Corden in *The Prom* and Armie Hammer in *Call Me by Your Name* prove, the old binaries still hold strong.

We should emphasise again that the stereotypes of gay men we see on television are a problem because of what they don't show, not necessarily because of what they show. Representations of stereotypically gay men are not in themselves a problem. There are groups whose cultural stereotypes include grossly negative qualities – Muslims as terrorists, black men as criminals – but there is nothing intrinsically negative about a feminine man. The feminine gay man, like the masculine gay woman or the trans person who fails to pass in a way that satisfies us, is only seen negatively because they are openly transgressing our sense of 'natural' gender roles. And in a society in which men continue to hold power over women, what could be more subversive than the man who chooses to squander his masculine power?

What is truly negative about the way feminine gay men are generally presented in film and on TV is that they are not afforded complex emotional inner lives. They are not allowed to be the romantic centre of their stories. All of the great gay romances in mainstream films, from *Brokeback Mountain* to *Call Me by Your Name*, involve two straight actors playing gay men as straight men. Again, these performances reflect truths – there are plenty of 'straight-acting'* gay men who fall in love. But in popular culture, these straight romances are not balanced out by romances centred on any gay men who don't pass as straight.

People talk about the comedy series *Schitt's Creek* as radical for presenting a gay relationship like any other relationship. But in fact what makes it radical is that the central romance involves David Rose, a main character who isn't a 'straight-acting' gay man. People talk about *RuPaul's Drag Race* as being radical in its presentation of the drag community. But what is truly radical about the show is that it presents feminine gay men, non-binary queens and trans women as complex emotional people. Because the show was made by gay men who intended the show only to be seen by other gay men, their

---

* It goes without saying that the term 'straight-acting' is particularly unfortunate, because it implies that the qualities we normally associate with masculine straight men are qualities that are being 'performed' in gay men who do not read as gay men and that, if they were not performing, they would read as stereotypically gay. It also implies that the qualities we normally associate with straightness are inherent in straight people. While many gay men are beautifully camp, so too are countless straight men and women. Russell Brand, Noel Fielding, Jack Black, Robin Williams, Jim Carrey, Jack Whitehall, Liza Minnelli, Goldie Hawn, Kim Cattrall, Tracee Ellis Ross, Amy Sedaris, Wendy Williams ... the list is endless.

language, their discussion of gay sex and gay lives, reaches us unfiltered. And it is all the more riveting for it.

Susan Sontag defined the essence of camp as 'its love of the unnatural: of artifice and exaggeration'.[5] But that does not mean that the camp gay man is unnatural or artificial; rather his campness reflects his recognition of the artificiality in how we all present ourselves, whether or not that presentation is considered 'natural'.

## It's Only Natural

The notion of a binary world in which some things are natural and others unnatural is a favourite argument of the homophobe, particularly when it comes to same-sex parenthood. 'A normal family is a man and a woman,' Israel's Education Minister said just last year, '[we] don't need to be ashamed that we live in this natural way.'[6] Throughout the world, religious texts and statute books decry sex between men as 'crimes against nature', with numerous former British colonies, from Pakistan to Uganda, still retaining the penal code against 'unnatural offences' gifted to them by Great Britain during the nineteenth century.

The most obvious problem with these laws and dictates is that in every conceivable definition of the word, homosexuality is natural. It is without question a product of nature. From gentoo penguins to spider monkeys, flamingos to bats, same-sex intercourse has been observed in over a thousand species.[7] Same-sex parenting is also common among species including swans and penguins; around 30 per cent of female albatrosses raise chicks in lifelong same-sex pairings.[8]

Even if this wasn't the case, homosexuality and same-sex families would still be natural simply by being an observable behaviour in humans. In one of his final essays, 'On Nature', John Stuart Mill says that nature in 'the abstract is the aggregate of the powers and properties of all things'. He goes on:

> Art is as much Nature as anything else; and everything which is artificial is natural – Art has no independent powers of its own: Art is but the employment of the powers of Nature for an end. Phenomena produced by human agency, no less than those which as far as we are concerned are spontaneous, depend on the properties of the elementary forces, or of the elementary substances and their compounds. The united powers of the whole human race could not create a new property of matter in general, or of any one of its species. [...] Even the volition which designs, the intelligence which contrives, and the muscular force which executes these movements, are themselves powers of Nature.[9]

In other words, humans are of nature and what they create and what they do is consequently natural. No other creature writes, but we don't consider writing unnatural because we've never seen our cat doing it. Indeed, we also never see our cat getting married. Straight marriage is solely a human activity and is thus only natural in the sense that tennis or break dancing is natural.

The naturalness of same-sex relationships is not just a philosophical and zoological given, it is historically proven too. Although the way we name and conceive of same-sex relationships has changed throughout history, records of same-sex attraction go back as far as we have historical records.[10]

Many international and historical laws against homosexuality have referred specifically to sodomy (interpreted usually as anal sex, although technically sodomy is any non-procreative sexual activity) as the key, punishable act that is 'against nature'. But in what sense is anal sex unnatural? Nature – or nature as guided by a creator, if that is your belief system – is incredibly good at stopping us being able to physically harm ourselves. See how far you can get your finger into your ear or your toe up your nose. If there was a creator who wanted to make sure we never engaged in anal sex, wouldn't they have just made our anuses the size of our nostrils?

It also makes no sense for anal sex to be repeatedly cited as the most incriminating act for homosexuality, because few gay women engage in it and laws truly aiming to stamp out sodomy would be squarely aimed at straight people. Anal sex is in fact third on the list of sexual acts that most gay men engage in most often, after oral sex and mutual masturbation. Twenty per cent of gay men never engage in anal sex, and some studies suggest that of the 80 per cent of gay men who have engaged in anal sex, only 38 per cent do so regularly.[11] With gay men representing around 3 per cent of the population and with around 40 per cent of straight people having engaged in anal sex, it is a sexual act that occurs far more often as an act of heterosexual sex.[12]

The idea of heterosexuality as natural and the heterosexual family as the natural family form feeds off our fetishisation of the idea of nature. Natural things are positive things. Natural births, natural skincare, natural materials. But rabies is also natural. Blood poisoning. Lockjaw. Psychosis.

Whenever you read about people wanting a natural death or a natural funeral you conjure up, perhaps, someone gently perspiring beneath an apple tree in the lap of a kaftan-clad death doula and being buried in a wicker coffin in a meadow. But that's not how animals die. A natural death is having your head bitten off by your sex partner or being eaten by an orca after they've tossed you around in the surf for a few hours. A natural funeral – that is to say, a funeral untouched by human cultural practices – would involve your body bloating where it fell until it was devoured by wild animals.

The argument that something is natural or unnatural is like the argument that something is just 'common sense'. We are simply saying, it's like that because it was always like that. We don't do it that way because most people don't do it that way. And we're too frightened to do it differently. It is what the Scottish philosopher David Hume described as the 'is–ought problem' – the mistake of believing that that which *is* is necessarily that which *ought* to be.[13]

When Tom told me back in 2006 that he wanted kids, it struck me as unnatural. I searched my mind for a picture of what he was talking about and turned up nothing. When he described to me his image of a perfect future, with a kid, a dog and a house, I literally saw it like a child's drawing. House with a door and two windows, a crayon spiral of smoke coming out of the chimney; Tom and me as stick men, our child with a huge pencil grin. My first tentative attempt to sketch a picture of what a queer family might look like with nothing to base it on.

What coloured in that picture, what changed it from a drawing to a photograph, to moving images – scenes of laughter around a kitchen table, a warmly lit room with a man humming to his baby, a sleepy Sunday on a sofa watching an unchallenging film – was meeting gay men and women who'd got married, who had kids, who were banally betrothed. It was as simple as that.


## Good Advice

While summarising my discovery that I was a gay man, I skipped an important detail: the two years, from seventeen to nineteen, that I had a girlfriend. I was, as I said, certain from the age of thirteen that I was gay. But with no chance of romance for a good half decade, and in need of cover, I dated a few girls in a very casual way, including my last girlfriend, Kinvara. Then, to my very great surprise, I fell in love with her. We were together for two years until she left me. I was heartbroken.

I'm aware that it's not a typical story, but it's certainly a simple one. And yet, time and time again, friends would tell my story back to me wrong. In a bar, at a party, if someone asked who Kinvara was, I would hear someone else say, 'Oh, it's Ben's ex. Who he dated before he realised he was gay.'

There were variations on the exact details, but the core tenet was: Ben thought he was straight, he dated a woman for two years, then he worked out he was gay and left her.

There's nothing wrong with that story. That's a story that's been played out many times, I'm sure. But it's not my story. There has not been a single moment since I was thirteen in which I thought I was straight, even when I was dating Kinvara. But I was in love with her and as attracted to her as fully as anybody I've been attracted to. And yet, at some deep level, people were so uncomfortable with that story that they subconsciously rewrote it.*

This really upset me because I felt it failed to honour what had been, at the time, the most important romantic

---

* It is interesting to think about how you would read this story if the genders were switched. Imagine that I'd told you I was a heterosexual man, married to a woman, and that for two years I'd gone out with a man. How would you read that story differently? Perhaps you wouldn't jump to the most extreme conclusion – that I was closeted and secretly gay – but you would certainly describe me as bisexual. On the basis of a relationship with a member of the same sex, David Bowie is considered bisexual in a way that, for instance, Gillian Anderson is not. Elton John, in our understanding, is clearly a gay man who was married to a woman, whereas Cynthia Nixon is a bisexual woman who was married to a man and is now married to a woman.

relationship of my life. I started telling people I was bisexual, not because I wanted to date women too after we'd broken up, but because I wanted people to recognise that my relationship with Kinvara was a proper relationship.

When I told Kinvara I was struggling with people misrepresenting it, she said, 'But I know it was real and you know it was real. That's all that matters.' She was right, of course, and I stopped worrying about it.

The fact that we were able to remain friends was in part due to some other good advice I got. Just after we broke up, I saw a university counsellor and she told me that, because we hadn't split up on equal terms – I had been left – my ex-girlfriend and I would never be able to remain friends. It was impossible. Those relationships never worked.

Being an eighteen-year-old student, I assumed that this middle-aged counsellor must know what she was talking about and I was devastated. I called Kinvara and told her, and she was in tears too. But a few days later I called my gran on her seventy-eighth birthday. She asked how Kinvara was – she was very fond of her – and I told her we'd broken up and related the story of the counsellor.

'She said we couldn't be friends. That it never works.'

'Then you be the first to make it work,' Gran said.

Simple as that.

She talked about meeting my grandfather during the war. He was twelve years older than her and about to get divorced. Her family and all of her friends said that those sort of relationships never worked, but she was sure it would. 'I just thought, it doesn't matter if it didn't work for anyone else,' she said, 'I'm going to make it work for us.' And she did.

Over the last few years, ever since Tom and I began to seriously explore the different ways in which we might become fathers, I've hungrily searched for images and stories of same-sex families to help build a solid foundation for the dreams of our future. And every time I've drawn a blank, I think about my gran saying, 'Then you be the first to make it work.' And I think about Kinvara and the first time I placed her godson in her arms.

# 3

# Hannah

## The Family We Never Had

In 2014, eight years after we first met, Tom and I had reached an impasse in our family planning. We were living in London, both working full time, commuting, never getting home earlier than seven. I was crawling out of bed an hour early to work on my second novel. Our weeks were tilted towards the weekend, which we spent recovering from the working week by drinking, eating and sleeping in. Our scant earnings were disappearing into our rent and the consolations we sought for our stressful weeks: food, booze, weekends away, trips back to Germany to see friends and Tom's family.

We had been to a number of adoption information sessions and met lots of enthusiastic social workers and parents-to-be. But every time we got home we would sit together, red wine in hand, in our living-room-cum-dining-room-cum-kitchen and try to fathom how we would bring up a happy child in our tiny flat with no extra cash and jobs that required our full attention.

I imagined taking our child to nursery at seven in the morning, me jacked up on caffeine as I pushed their buggy through the grey streets, then returning home twelve hours later to kiss them goodnight. I didn't want to be a weekend dad, but I couldn't see any route out of it without making some sort of major change to our lives.

Then Tom got a call from an old colleague in Berlin who had a successful therapy practice and wanted someone to come and share her growing list of clients. She was wondering whether Tom might be interested. The earnings would be enough to support a family even working part time, she told us; she had done the same with her two kids.

Tom and I had already lived in Berlin for three years when we were first together. We loved it, but we also loved England, and when we moved back to the UK in 2011 we believed that we were moving back for good. The bigger issue was that, when Tom's colleague called three years later, adoption in Germany for same-sex couples was not a possibility and wasn't even on the cards politically.

The only option available to us in Germany would have been what is termed long-term foster care, which would have required us to have monthly contact with a child's birth parents. That wasn't a problem emotionally, but practically it would have meant that we may have been required to get permission from the child's birth parents whenever we wanted to leave the country. Not ideal for an Anglo-German family with a set of grandparents, aunts and uncles overseas.

'What about having a child with Hannah?' Tom said.

The suggestion hadn't come from nowhere. She was a very old friend of Tom's, a speech therapist who also lived in Berlin. She was in her late thirties and there'd been some drunken imaginings at someone's wedding a few years earlier of what it would be like to have a family together.

'I suppose,' I said. Tom and I were sitting in the living room with a cup of tea, our socked feet touching on the coffee table.

It was another of those moments in which I was met with a suggestion that I hadn't ever seriously considered. And so I didn't really know how I felt about it.

'I mean, in one sense it's more complicated. We'll be tied together as a family. But in another way it's much easier. We just have to provide some sperm.'

It was true. Throughout our exploration into adoption we had been grappling with the complex bureaucracy. Suddenly there seemed to be something very simple about just getting someone pregnant. Something liberating and adventurous. I didn't know anyone who'd created a family among friends and it sounded like a beautiful thing to do. I imagined the three of us at some family garden party, walking barefoot through the grass, our blissful chubby child in Hannah's arms, its face happily stained with fruit and dirt.

'If anyone could make it work . . .' I said.

Tom nodded.

This wasn't the first conversation that Tom and I had had with a female friend about the concept of starting a family. In fact we'd had plenty of similar conversations before we'd even met. We had both experienced numerous drunken evenings with close female friends that ended with us sunk deep into some ancient sofa holding hands and promising each other that, if we ever got to thirty-five – which seemed so old and so impossibly distant to us back then – we would have a kid with each other.

And anyway, we would say with drunken seriousness, our teeth edged in purple, wouldn't it actually be sublime? Wouldn't it actually be better than a 'normal' family? Just parental love and none of that failed romance shit. We would never split up because we would never have been romantically involved. We'd have responsibility and freedom. We almost couldn't wait.

All of these female friends found partners, of course. And

many of them disappeared altogether once they had had children. This was the risk of such an arrangement. That we would always be the back-up plan. Whereas for us, there was no social or personal expectation of what our family was meant to look like, for these female friends we would at best always be a good consolation prize.

## A Child of My Very Own

It wasn't that it was completely impossible for Tom and me to raise biological children on our own. There was surrogacy, of course. But for us, the question of our child being biologically related to us had never seemed very important. This was a feeling. Initially, it didn't stem from any kind of in-depth moral thinking around the benefits of adoption. It was just in our respective guts.

I would certainly not have been against having my own biological children had the option been as simple as it is for straight couples. After over a decade of exploring and working through various strategies to create a family, I am often stunned when straight friends tell me their conception stories. 'We got drunk at Natalie's wedding and forgot to use a condom.' 'We just kind of didn't try *not* to get pregnant.' 'I stopped taking the pill and, *bam!*'

What bliss.

Having biological children as a gay couple, though, is not simple. It is a process with different complexities to adoption, but complexities none the less. For a start, surrogacy is legally limited in both the UK and Germany, meaning you can't pay someone to carry your child. And in the USA, where surrogacy is legal and which is the most common surrogacy destination for parents in the latter countries, it costs around £100,000.

The high cost of surrogacy opens up other moral obstacles. Gay couples who are forced to pick more affordable routes to surrogacy in, say, Ukraine or Georgia have to grapple with the same ethical concerns that haunt international adoption – that, without very strict legal oversight, the exchange of money in the founding of any family always has the potential to skew the power dynamics to the detriment of the birth mother in the poorer country.

When wealthy Western Europeans are paying for surrogacy in a country like Ukraine, the young surrogate mothers in question will often be paid almost £16,000 – eight times the average annual income in that country.[1] This would be like an American surrogate being paid almost half a million dollars to carry a child. Even if the surrogacy markets in Eastern Europe were free from corruption – and there is no evidence that they are – you still have to wrestle with the extent to which mothers living in poverty are making an unbiased decision about their bodies and the children they carry.

If gay fathers do manage to pick their way through these very real concerns, ensuring as they go that the surrogate mother in question is indeed freely choosing to help them start a family, then they are still forced to face a series of moral criticisms that adoptive fathers – and certainly straight parents – generally avoid.

The chief criticism laid at the doors of gay men using surrogates is that they are being selfish trying to bag a biological child of their own, especially in countries like the UK and the USA in which there are thousands of children in need of adoption and fostering.[2]

On this populous planet of dwindling resources, you could of course level this criticism at anyone choosing to have their own biological children. We generally accept straight couples paying tens of thousands on fertility treatment when they are unable to conceive; we do not accuse them of selfishness for abandoning the children they might have fostered or adopted.

Indeed, even in the United States where surrogacy is legal, only around two thousand children are born to surrogates every year, and over half of those are to international couples.[3] If every new American surrogate family – gay or straight – adopted last year it would have barely scratched the surface of the 117,000 children waiting to be adopted in the USA.[4]

Gay surrogate fathers are also accused of being implicated in the absence of their child's mother; of engineering a situation in which their child is motherless. The role of homophobia in this reproof is revealed in how often surrogacy arrangements are questioned when they involve Elton John or Tom Daley, and how rarely when they involve celebrity mothers in straight relationships, like Nicole Kidman or Sarah Jessica Parker.[5]

This 'absent parent' argument also reveals how little we value biological fathers when critiquing reproductive interventions. In the USA, up to 60,000 children are officially born each year using sperm donors, and this is likely to be an underestimate; that's thirty times higher than the number of surrogate births in the USA.[6] Yet there are five times as many scholarly articles published on the ethics of surrogacy compared to the ethics of sperm donation.[7]

The research that we do have on the children of surrogates suggests that they are well adjusted and feel very positively towards the surrogate that carried them.[8] There are many children of anonymous sperm donors, on the other hand, who feel deeply ambivalent about having no knowledge about or connection to their biological father, while also feeling that those concerns are largely dismissed by society.[9] And if they do wish to find out who their biological father is, the lack of regulation in the industry often makes this almost impossible.

\*

Much discussed and much maligned, surrogacy remains in fact a very atypical way for parents – gay or straight – to start a family. It entails ethical hurdles, but these hurdles exist and are underexplored in the myriad more common ways of starting a family with reproductive assistance – from egg and sperm donation to egg freezing and IVF.

For Tom and me, these hurdles were too great when we had never planned for biology to play a part in our family equation. Adoption, for us, had always been the dream. That was until Tom suggested the idea of starting a family with Hannah. But here the pull for us was again not biology but simplicity. What could be easier than just turning up at someone's flat one evening with a turkey baster and a bottle of red wine, ready to make a baby?

## Not for My Sake

Hannah is, in many ways, an ur-Berliner. She grew up in Bremen – not being from Berlin is very Berlin – and she studied abroad, coming to Berlin because so many of her friends from so many important moments in her life had ended up there. She does yoga, she meditates, she smokes. She grows strawberries on her balcony. She drinks the hard Pils of northern Germany; the Helles of the south she finds too sweet. She has no television, but watches films and British and American series on her laptop, and she reads voraciously. She sews her own soft-furnishings. She knits hats, socks and scarves for friends. She cycles everywhere on an ancient unbranded Dutch bike, has a share in an allotment and makes potent, almost dung-smelling coffee in a matt aluminium moka pot.

Her flat is a perfect Berlin flat. The rooms are huge, her

bed and the giant Ikea wardrobe lost at the edge of a sea of varnished floorboards. The bathroom is narrow and dim with those old German toilets that have a little shelf in them so that you can inspect your stool after defecation. There is no living room.* The kitchen is not fitted but made up of a series of mismatched cupboards and white goods accrued over decades by former tenants. The dishwasher is from the 1980s. The work surface is made up of a terrace of wooden boards screwed together haphazardly. Spider plants, cheese plants, jade trees fill shelves, and nest atop the nostalgic 1930s glazed dresser that contains mismatched cutlery and crockery gathered from flea markets and left behind at parties.

Before we moved, we sat around the table that fills most of the space in the kitchen; we ate lentil curry by candlelight, drank beer and then wine, and discussed the baby we were going to have together. These were no longer imaginary conversations. We carefully outlined our worries. We didn't want to be Sunday dads. When it came to important decisions, like vaccinations and schools, we wanted to make them as a threesome, not just be consulted.

Our biggest worry at the time was about a potential stepfather. A man that Hannah might one day meet who was going to be a step-parent to our child. 'I may never meet anyone,' Hannah said. But she had never been single for more than a year or so; at some point there was probably going to be another man.

Despite the concrete nature of our discussions, Hannah intermittently became worried and would interrupt us to say, 'But don't move for me. I can't be responsible for you moving to Berlin. What if it didn't work out? I mean, I might not even get pregnant.'

---

* The supremacy of the living room, it turns out, is a very Anglo-Saxon concept. In Berlin, in Germany as a whole, life revolves around the kitchen table.

'But how are we going to start a family if we don't move?' we might have said. But we didn't. We said, 'You're not the only reason we're moving back to Berlin. There's Tom's job.' And Tom's job did matter, but Tom had a job in London. We were moving for the possibility of parenthood.

Hannah's imagined future partner became a faceless figure in my picture of our future and a source of anxiety for me. This man who, if he loved Hannah in the way that I hoped she would be loved, would also love our child. And if that man loved our child, he would become a third father in our child's life and no more or less that child's father than I would be if it wasn't my sperm that we ended up using; because you can't legally have more than two parents at a time in Germany, this man would have exactly the same claim on our child as I did. And if Hannah and he got married, he might even have more.

'And what if that man wanted to move to Australia?'

'I don't want to move to Australia,' Hannah said.

But if he was perfect? I thought. Were we enough to keep her in Berlin?

Hannah voiced many worries too, particularly about the weight of two against one in our parenting relationships. She worried that in all decisions Tom and I would be unified and she would always be in the minority.

I felt that motherhood would weigh in her favour. I wondered if it wouldn't end up giving her a veto. I couldn't imagine that, if push came to shove, we were going to end up forcing her to vaccinate her child if she didn't want them to be vaccinated. If our opinions differed from hers on breastfeeding or co-sleeping, those opinions would be pretty irrelevant.

I didn't say any of this though. Generally, I felt that the scales tipped towards her in these discussions, because she was giving more up in our arrangement than we were. We were making sacrifices, not least moving back to Berlin and tying ourselves to the city. But we were also giving up being parents together as a couple.

And yet, we didn't have to give up on any kind of romantic dream; we already had each other. Hannah would have to give up a dream. At a time when she still could give birth naturally and in which there was still a shrinking window of opportunity to meet 'the one', she'd have to give up the dream of a nuclear family, of having the children of the man she loved. If she did meet the love of her life after she got pregnant, she could still build a wonderful life with him, but it would be a different kind of life, with two other parents to deal with.

Hannah worried that we wouldn't be able to care for her after she had the child in the way that someone she was romantically involved with would care for her.

'Of course we'll care for you,' I said.

But I was also thinking that we couldn't care for her like that. We could look after her and always be present. But if, say, she needed to be held weeping through the night after a miscarriage, then we would be asleep in another flat and she would be alone in her sorrow. We wouldn't be able to comfort her the way a partner might.

There was great hope for the family we wanted to build, though, and I feel nostalgic for that hope. There were risks, concerns on both sides that weren't being voiced as honestly as they should've been. But there was also the prospect of giving a child three parents who loved them completely. There was the prospect of all the intensity of parenthood with some blessed relief. The possibility of Hannah or us being able to fly off for a week without feeling like we were leaving someone else in the lurch. The possibility of lie-ins, of free weekends, of the work of parenting, so often shouldered by one person, being shouldered not by two parents, but by three. All the benefits of the divorcee's mix of freedom and responsibility without the terrible destructive force of divorce. In some ways, it all sounded too good to be true.

## Risky Business

Other friends gently pointed out the risks of having a child with someone you're not going out with. But my and Tom's relationship is the result of a series of great risks taken for love. We met at a friend's birthday party when we were in our mid-twenties. It was a disco and funk night at a bar in Holborn called Brown Sugar. My friend Toby had fallen for a glamorous German girl who had recently moved to London from New York and he had heard that she was going to be at the party. But when she turned up, she was accompanied by two handsome friends from back home.

'Do you think she's dating one of them?' Toby asked me.

I had my doubts.

I had arrived at the party pretty drunk and when I managed to get chatting to Tom – one of the handsome friends from back home – I felt like we had a great connection and was convinced I was being very charming. I remember his wonderful smile and saying to myself in my head, 'You have definitely pulled, Ben. This is a sure thing.'

At the end of the night, we wandered off with our friends to find something to eat. Beneath the blueish strip-lighting of a kebab shop on Old Compton Street, he invited me back to a friend's flat, which, in my drunken state, I thought was his flat.

We sat around in what was in fact his friend's living room drinking whisky and listening to 'Love Hangover' by Diana Ross. Someone rolled a joint, and although I had never even smoked cigarettes I gamely took drag after drag as the joint was passed round, not wishing to lose any of the apparent mystique I had built up in this lovely German's eyes.

In a film of this evening we would now hard-cut to curtains being pulled open and pale London sunshine piercing the dark space, revealing a billion dancing smuts of golden dust. I was fully dressed, woken where I had been lying on the sofa with my whisky glass unmoved.

'Did I fall asleep?'

Tom was standing between me and the window. 'You could not be budged. I tried to wake you a couple of times, but you were out cold.'

'Shit,' I said. 'Sorry.'

He was smiling. 'I'm going home now.'

'Oh,' I said. 'Where's home?'

'Bonn.'

'Bonn in Germany?' I said as a joke. I thought it was some cool new neighbourhood east of Hackney that I'd never heard of.

He nodded though. We hadn't even kissed.

For a week, my failure was just another classic tale from what had been a rather dry period in my life, romantically. But then Tom sent me a text message. He'd got my number from Christine (the glamorous blonde German who did live in London)* and was going to be over twice in October visiting her and Seb (the other handsome friend), and would I like to meet up?

This was a lie. He had booked those trips to come and see me, because, despite my failure to even hold his hand, he was convinced that I was the one.

After a year and a half of dating long-distance between London and Berlin I quit my job and moved to Germany. 'Quite risky,' a few friends said. But it really didn't feel risky

---

* I should add that Toby won Christine over and they're now married with two kids.

to me. I just knew it would work out. And we had three wonderful years, before we moved back to London in 2011.

So the idea of returning to Berlin to start a family with Hannah seemed like just another one of those risks. I understood my friends' concern, but I knew a good thing when I saw it. I was convinced we'd be fine.

## The Cameraman

So Tom and I moved back to Berlin. We lived at Hannah's flat for the first six weeks while we were looking for our own flat. Among the usual stresses of setting up bank accounts, registering addresses and arranging health insurance, we had some very cosy times together. Because Tom was already Hannah's friend, Hannah and I tried to do some things on our own. I cooked dinner for her when Tom was out, we went to the cinema. We got on well during those six weeks and she was sad about how quickly we had found a flat.

It was a great six weeks, but I felt very happy to have found a flat and to have space for just Tom and me again. I did worry a little that the whole thing wasn't going to work out; Tom was much more confident. If I had a worry about it working out, it was mainly the intimacy that the relationship would entail. It was the inevitable requirement for me to be emotionally open, to be vulnerable and intimate with a woman who was a friend, but not my close friend, and certainly not my lover.

Throughout that winter we returned to Hannah's kitchen and discussed the practicalities of making a baby. Whose sperm should we use? Maybe it would be better for it to be Tom's, we thought, because they're old friends. But then a friend of Hannah's said, 'Maybe that's exactly why it should be Ben's sperm and not Tom's.'

I worried about the quality of my sperm, about presenting it on the day of insemination only to discover that it didn't work. That it was defective. And how were we going to hand it over? In a glass? An egg cup? On a spoon? I imagined Tom and Hannah waiting in the kitchen while I masturbated in the toilet, the deed done behind a closed door, like that TV show in which people have sex in a box and then sheepishly come out to talk about it with Mariella Frostrup.

We discussed mixing the sperm together, so that we wouldn't know who the biological father was. It was a sweet thought. But then we pictured the four of us, our child with her English potato face and mousey hair and us earnestly saying, 'We have no idea who the father is.'

Hannah was still going on dates at this time. On the way back from her flat Tom and I often talked about whether we should be worried about it. We felt it was inappropriate to tell her we didn't like that she was going on dates. But we also didn't like that she was going on dates.

She told us that it was completely separate from what we were doing, but we couldn't really understand how. A female friend told us that we should tell her she couldn't date anyone until the baby arrived. But two men telling a woman who she can and can't have sex with? That felt very wrong, and we didn't say anything.

Hannah downloaded an app that let us work out exactly when she'd be ovulating. She told us that she'd started sleeping with an old friend she'd known for years – a cameraman. 'It's not a relationship, it's just sex, and we shouldn't change our plans.'

We became worried, though, but we kept making plans. We worked out which of our flats we were going to be in during the first months of our baby's life and in spring we went through our diaries to pick a provisional date for the first insemination. April, we thought.

'I've got a holiday pencilled in and I want to drink,' she said, so we agreed on June.

The holiday was with another couple and the cameraman.

'Sounds like a couples' holiday?' I said, in a jokey way.

'Oh no,' she said. 'It's just a group of friends.'

We met up when she got back. In the heat of summer, Berlin was transformed. The city was living on the streets, the cafés emptying their furniture onto the pavements, tables levelled out on the cobbles with folded beer mats, children clattering past on tricycles, scooters and bikes. Evening sun gilded the pastel facades of the buildings, illuminating Berliners on their balconies, smoking and drinking, watering their tomato plants.

For some reason – perhaps because everywhere else was full – we picked a café that we often passed but never went into, because it was always suspiciously empty. It was a 'fashion café' where you could buy coffee, cake, a beer, but also dresses made by the owner. Berlin is full of these kinds of café that seem to be fulfilling someone's dream of a café but are trying to do too many things at once and so never have any customers. In any other city, they would close after a few weeks. But in Berlin the owners have an old rental agreement, can survive on selling a few cups of coffee a day, a slice of yesterday's *Streuselkuchen* and – in this case – a skirt every month or two.

We sat outside on benches, glossy and white like picket fences, drinking beer. The owner's ancient snaggle-toothed French bulldog shuffled out to sniff around at our feet.

'Something changed while we were on holiday,' Hannah said. 'I didn't think it would, but I've really fallen for him. And I think I need to see where it's going to go.'

It was exactly what we feared was going to happen, which somehow made it more devastating. At least a clean shock that comes out of nowhere has a sort of sparky freshness as it knocks you sideways. But something crumbling that you thought was crumbling – that is especially crushing.

'I just want to put it on hold and see how it goes.'

'And what are we meant to do?' I said.

'Just wait.'

I sipped my beer. 'But I don't just want to wait in the hope that you'll break up with him. I don't want to be sitting about praying for your relationship to fail.'

There wasn't an answer to this. The owner of the café, an elegant Turkish-German woman with wild greying hair and a pale home-made dress, asked us if we'd like to order anything else. We shook our heads.

At the beginning of September, we agreed to meet up to have a final conversation, though I didn't know what we were going to talk about. We ate parmigiana and drank red wine in the same kitchen she had welcomed us to when we had triumphantly returned to Berlin a year before. As we went over everything we had already said at the café, I felt that she was trying to unpick the narrative of the last year. She kept talking about 'the idea we'd been chatting about' rather than 'the plans we had made'.

I began to question myself. Had I been fooling myself all along? And this is still what upsets me most. This unravelling of the dream we had shared for eighteen months, had carried from London to Berlin, this hollowing out of our imagined family, so that we couldn't even say goodbye to it together.

I was in tears; we all were. It felt like a break-up.

'But we really meant it,' I kept saying.

'I meant it too,' she said to me. But how could she have done?

## A Reckoning

This is, of course, my memory of what happened to us that year. I have no doubt that Hannah tells a different story just as true and just as false.

I still feel hurt. I am an emotional person, but not a very emotionally open person. I don't like being vulnerable in front of anyone except for my husband, not even my family, not even my friends. I felt like I was emotionally open with Hannah and that it was a mistake. It reminded me of a trick that a boy once played on me at school, opening his arms as if to hug me and when I opened my arms to hug him back he punched me in the stomach. I felt ashamed then about what I'd let happen and I feel ashamed now about what I let happen with Hannah.

Funnily enough, it is not the move back to Berlin that I regret. What I regret is not being completely honest about our worries. In her moments of doubt, I felt that Hannah wanted and needed us to be entirely confident and consoling in our promises. We were afraid that if we were not completely positive about our plan together we might scare Hannah off. But that's exactly what we should have been braver about.

The main driver of our move to Berlin was to start a family with Hannah. But we kept telling her that that was just one reason among many and she didn't have to feel any pressure about it. What we should have said was, 'The main reason we're moving to Berlin is to start this family with you that we've been talking about having.' If Hannah had then said no, if she had said that she couldn't handle the pressure of us moving just for that, then we shouldn't have moved.

When she began dating, we should have said, 'We're really uncomfortable with you dating while we're trying to start this family.' If she'd said – as she would have completely had the right to – 'That's bullshit. I'm not about to start a family with two men who tell me who I can and can't date,' then our plan would have broken down on honest terms.

She was telling us before we moved and when she started dating that she was not as invested in the plan as we were. But we were too afraid of losing our dream of a family by listening to what she was actually saying.

## Nietzschean Regrets

Of course, without the breakdown of that plan, we would not have our son. We didn't know this at the time, though. There were months after the plan had collapsed in which Tom and I were sure we would never have a family. But five years on, as sore as I still am about what happened, I don't regret that we went through it.

'You see,' friends said to me in the months after Theo arrived, 'everything happens for a reason.'

I would like to buy into this thought. And it is tempting. Theo is theoretically the answer to every regret I ever had up until the day he arrived. Because if I had made any number of decisions differently in my life Tom and I wouldn't have met Theo in Berlin on that mild October morning.

The only problem is that I don't believe in this kind of active fate. I used to believe in it. I used to be vaguely convinced that every negative thing that happened to you happened for a reason. That it had the potential to be a moment of learning.

The experience that killed this feeling for me was the friend of mine who got cancer at twenty-nine. She survived; she is now cancer-free and happily married with kids. But it was the first time in my life that I had witnessed someone going through something which had no ostensible benefit. I had no silver-lining spiel for her. Getting cancer in the midst of her youth was just terrible. She lost two years of her life going through surgery, radiotherapy and chemotherapy. She lost her job, she lost friends. It left scars in and on her body that she will live with for the rest of her life. In a world with any rightness in it, it should never have happened to her.

How does one square the great fortunes of life with these great disasters if one doesn't believe that everything happens for a reason? I am most convinced by Friedrich Nietzsche's concept of *amor fati*, or love of fate. In *Ecce Homo*, in the bravely titled chapter 'Why I Am So Clever', Nietzsche writes: 'My formula for human greatness is *amor fati*: not wanting anything to be different, not forwards, not backwards, not for all eternity. Not just enduring what is necessary, still less concealing it (all idealism is hypocrisy in the face of what is necessary), but *loving* it . . .'[10]

Nietzsche is not suggesting that we pretend to be happy about the bad things that happen to us. Nor is he suggesting that we take whatever life throws at us lying down. What he is saying is that we should radically love our lives for what they are, good and bad, not what we wish them to have been.

Is it possible to love our lives in this way? We know it is, because it is the way that we love our children. It is the way that we love their lives. Our rage at their misdeeds and our ecstasy at their joys is uncoupled from a deep river of affection that flows endlessly beneath our relationships with them. It is this deep affection that we should be attempting to channel beneath our own lives when we reflect on our own fates and failures. Appalled by the lows, overjoyed by the highs, but always feeling a deep love for our unchangeable fates.

# 4

# Parent School

## Step-child Adoption

When we first made the call to the adoption agency in Berlin the chances of us adopting were very slim. We made the call, in fact, just before adoption was legalised for same-sex couples on the basis of one friend who knew a same-sex couple who had managed to adopt in Berlin through what was called 'step-child adoption'.

In Germany, only married couples are allowed to adopt and, until 2017, same-sex couples could enter into civil partnerships, but not marry. There was one rarely used loophole: a law originally designed to allow same-sex partners to become the legal parent of their partner's biological children from a previous relationship. In exceptional circumstances, more liberal states in Germany had occasionally allowed one partner to adopt a child as a single person and then their partner to adopt what was now technically their partner's legal offspring. It was lawful, but only allowed at the discretion of social services and judges in extremely rare cases in which it was clear that there was no other option for the child.

To me, the odds just seemed impossible. It was hard enough

to adopt a child if you were a straight married couple. I didn't see how this friend of a friend was proof enough that we were going to have any chance of adopting in a system that was challenging for straight, married adopters, let alone gay adopters. My husband, though, is imbued with a magical combination of optimism and cheerful stubbornness that, after fifteen years of close observation, I have yet to see broken.

## You Oughta Know

A few years ago, my husband, a psychotherapist, wrote a self-help book. Having seen me go through the publishing process a few times he knew that there was a stage in which the book would be sent out for reviews. His suggestions for who should receive copies of my novels have always been stratospherically optimistic. 'What about Kazuo Ishiguro?' he would say. 'Or Margaret Atwood?'

'That's not how it works,' I would reply, looking forward to a time in the future in which he would try and publish his own book and realise how brutal the process really was.

'I've been thinking about who would be good to get a quote from for my book,' he said dreamily as we sat in bed drinking tea, staring at the tall ivy-clad acacias that swung precariously in the wind outside our bedroom window. 'And I was thinking of Alanis Morissette.'

I laughed. 'Maybe you should try Sting too.'

He smiled accommodatingly at my teasing, and a few days later appeared on the sofa with his laptop. 'I'm going to email this psychologist in California. I met her at a conference and she said she'd met Alanis. Can you read through what I've written just to make sure the tone isn't too pushy.'

I read through the email. 'I mean, it is a bit pushy.'

'But not rude.'

'Well, no.'

The psychologist in California emailed back to say that sending his book to Alanis was not appropriate and she didn't really know her that well. This response, which would have devastated me, was accepted sanguinely by my husband.

I gave him a knowing nod when he told me and said, 'Well, you tried your best. That's what counts.'

A few days later the psychologist emailed again to say that she'd been thinking about it and had come to the conclusion that it really wasn't for her to decide whether or not Alanis wanted to read the book. So she would email one of Alanis's assistants, whose details she still had, and ask her whether my husband could forward a proof copy of his book. A few days later the psychologist emailed the address of a PO box in California.

My husband wrapped up the book and included a handwritten note telling Alanis that he knew how interested she was in the topic. Watching him at the dining room table writing his note, I could imagine Tom as a teenager sending fan letters to the musicians he loved and I felt a mixture of love and, simultaneously, the same sort of almost enjoyable sadness you feel when you see something sweetly pitiful: a dog with three legs, or an old man eating perfectly cut sandwiches on a bench by himself.

For the next three months Tom would say, 'Do you think Alanis will get back to me this week?'

'You never know,' I would say cheerfully while loading the dishwasher.

'She's just had a baby, so she's probably busy.'

'Sure,' I would say, spitting my toothpaste into the sink. 'That's probably it. It's probably the baby.'

A few weeks later, he woke me up in the middle of the night. 'She texted,' he whispered, sounding pleased but unsurprised.

'Who texted?'

'Alanis Morissette. She's sent me a page on the book. We're going to edit it down on email tomorrow.'

## The Virtuoso

In February 2017, before same-sex marriage had been legalised in Germany, Tom let his powers of persuasion loose on Berlin's creaking bureaucracy. He called the adoption department in the Berlin Senate and was told that the odds were low, that they weren't taking on any new applicants at the moment and that we should look at other options.

He called back a month later to ask if anything had changed and managed to convince them to at least put our names on the list to be called back when they started taking new applicants again.

They didn't call back, so Tom phoned again and they agreed to send us some initial forms to fill out along with a list of documents we would need to provide if we were to be accepted onto the application programme. We returned our forms, but heard nothing more.

Then, in June 2017, something surprising happened.

For years, Angela Merkel's governing conservative CDU party had been knocking back attempts to legalise same-sex marriage in Germany by opposition parties in parliament. Merkel herself had commented that her 'gut feeling' was that marriage was between a man and a woman. At the beginning of 2017, the various opposition parties, including the SPD – the Social Democratic Party and the junior party in Merkel's coalition government – tried, unsuccessfully, to force a vote on a same-sex marriage bill.

This was an election year in Germany, and each of Merkel's

potential coalition partners – the SPD, the liberal FDP and the Greens – made statements saying that a bill on same-sex marriage would be a non-negotiable part of any coalition deal for government after the election. So even if the CDU was the largest party after the election, Merkel's new conservative government would be forced to agree to a bill on same-sex marriage.

Internationally, Merkel is often viewed as a solid, very capable and very reliable political operator. What people outside Germany often miss is that her success was grounded in how well she played the game of political risk at home.

She became head of the CDU party after becoming the first CDU politician to break ranks and publicly criticise her then boss, Chancellor Helmut Kohl, after he was implicated in a donations scandal in 1999. When the CDU scraped a win in the 2005 election, her opponent, Gerhard Schröder, publicly announced in her presence on election night that he would be the next Chancellor, because he commanded more support in parliament. Two months later Merkel formed her first government.

The vote on same-sex marriage was another Merkel coup de maître. To the surprise of her party, the opposition parties and the media, she announced during a public Q&A in Berlin that she believed there needed to be a conscience vote – i.e. a vote in which members of parliament were not forced to vote along party lines – on same-sex marriage. And that it should happen in the near future.

Just three days later, parliament had organised a conscience vote for the very last session before the summer recess. Merkel said she would vote against the bill, but not on moral grounds, only because she felt that marriage was defined as being between a man and a woman in the German constitution.

All of the major opposition parties voted for the legislation, as did seventy-five of Merkel's own MPs, meaning the bill easily passed with a majority of 62.4 per cent. The SPD and other opposition parties claimed the result as a victory.

But the real victor was Merkel. Realising that the opposition parties were going to use same-sex marriage as an election issue, she had called their bluff and allowed them to remove the issue from the table. She had appealed to liberal Germans by allowing the vote, while managing not to alienate herself with conservative voters by voting against the bill. But the reason she gave was no longer a 'gut feeling'; she claimed that she was voting against same-sex marriage on a dry point of constitutional law.

Merkel won the election. Her main opposition, the SPD, suffered the worst defeat of its post-war history.


## Roundtable

A month after Germany's new marriage law was enacted, allowing Tom and me to have our English marriage recognised in Germany, we finally got a call inviting us to an adoption information evening.

Adoption in Germany is run directly by the local authority rather than an agency. In Berlin, it is a branch of the Berlin Senate that organises adoptions from lino-clad offices in a palatial stone building of clattering corridors and endless glazed safety doors. At the information evening we sat around a huge polished table – redolent of the war room in *Dr Strangelove* – with fifty or so other couples. Others who had turned up late had to sit on chairs in the corridor.

'Let me start with the bitter pill,' the exhausted-looking social worker said to us, unclipping and reclipping a section of her wispy brown hair. She had the brisk no-nonsense air of a seasoned headteacher. 'Less than a hundred children a year are put up for adoption and we have a couple of thousand couples in our pool of prospective adopters. To get into this pool, you will need to go through a year-long process of monthly meetings and home visits. We only have three social workers in this department, who are also responsible for placing children and dealing with the mothers who are giving up their children for adoption. One of them is currently off sick. This means that we are currently taking *no* new applicants. If after this meeting you are still interested in continuing with an application, it is strongly recommended that you explore foster care, where more parents are needed. The likelihood is that most of you won't make it through.'

It felt like we were about to start training for the Hunger Games.

As she talked about the kinds of background children who are put up for adoption have, I looked around at the other people in the room. It was not a diverse crowd, mostly straight, mostly white. There was one other same-sex couple in the room, a little younger and a little more pristine than ourselves. I wondered if they or we would get through the process and, if we both did, who would be able to adopt first.

'Does anyone know what effects drinking can have on a foetus?' the social worker asked.

One half of the other gay couple put up his hand. 'Well,' he said, with a little faux embarrassment, 'as a *doctor*, I know that . . .'

Well, that settles that, I thought.

The social worker told us that most people drop out after this initial meeting and that many people don't make it all the way through the following series of meetings. Once parents realise the reality of what the adoption process entails they often can't offer the requisite commitment.

'Great,' Tom said as we left.

'Great? She basically said it was impossible.'

'No, she just said it was difficult.'

Four months later, after a little more prodding by Tom, we received a call to tell us that we could make an official application. But first we would need to collect a few documents.

## The Paper Trail

National stereotypes are generally overblown, are usually outdated and are often just plain wrong. For an Englishman in Germany, these stereotypes inevitably revolve around English food and English weather. In school in nineties West Germany, my husband was told that there wasn't such a thing as British food. I had a colleague tell me how disgusting British food was based on a full English breakfast she had eaten in New Zealand; she didn't like the maple syrup on the scrambled eggs, apparently. I have had people tell me, in the darkest depths of a Berlin winter, that they wouldn't travel to the UK because of the awful weather, while we were standing ankle deep in filthy snow with sleet in our ears at four in the afternoon when it was already pitch black.

In Britain, most of our favourite stereotypes about Germans are similarly misplaced. Germans are in fact pretty charming, certainly very funny. They laugh and smile a lot. They're very warm. The food in Germany is great, the wine is amazing, the summers are roasting hot. And all of Germans' actual national oddities – their primal fear of draughts; their obsession with airing rooms; their aversion to eating more than one warm meal a day* – are

---

\* If you're English, one of the oddest of German cultural oddities is 'Dinner for One', a black-and-white English-language comedy sketch from the 1960s which is shown every year on New Year's Eve. The film is almost completely unknown in the UK, but all Germans think that it is a British import and cultural touchstone. The famous line from the sketch, 'same procedure as last year', is so well known in Germany that you can use it in any situation in which you're going to repeat something in the same way as you usually do it. When I first moved to Berlin, people constantly winked at me and said 'same procedure as last year', and for about three years I had no idea what they were talking about.

largely unknown abroad. But one of the few national stereotypes that does stick is Germans' obsession with and reliance on an expansive and paper-based bureaucracy. And the adoption process, as you might imagine, is no exception.

German bureaucracy is the bureaucracy of your wildest bureaucratic dreams. Imagine that every time you needed a new passport, a new driver's licence, a copy of your marriage certificate or child's birth certificate, needed to move house even, you had to go to the town hall in person to register it. Imagine that this town hall was a nineteenth-century town hall of palace-like proportions. Imagine this palace filled with kilometre upon anonymous kilometre of lino-clad corridors, polished to a brilliant sheen. Imagine wandering these corridors for hours with your documents in your hand, the air filled with the scent of municipal liquid soap, ancient plumbing, damp plaster and a distant canteen, smelt and heard but never seen. The only other sound is the squeak of your shoes on that lino, the colour of which is so institutionally neutral that you couldn't even identify it. Green? Grey? Sky blue? Who could say? You search anxiously for Room 157 in Section C, but after Section B you find yourself in Section D. And when you find Section C, it's called Section C.1. and the rooms are numbered backwards from 300 and stop at 180. And when you finally find Room 157 – in Section C.2.1, which was on a mezzanine floor not shown on the floorplan – you knock and, receiving no answer, push at a giant wooden door, to be confronted by a room of people silently typing. One woman near the back of the room, who stares at you open-mouthed and slightly affronted beneath a wilting spider plant, then looks through your documents and informs you that they're incomplete. The next day, when you've retrieved the correct documents, your Kafkaesque journey will begin again.

In Germany you need a stamped piece of paper to do

anything. But there is a stamped piece of paper available for anything you might need to do. And you are legally obliged to present it. When I got my university job in Potsdam, I had to fill in sixteen different forms, the longest of which was thirty pages, and present certified copies of not only my degree certificates but also my A Levels and GCSEs. I didn't even know when I'd last seen my GCSE certificates, nor what any of them actually looked like.

When I told my German friend Michael about this he couldn't quite see what was so odd about it. 'But how else would they know whether you'd got the grades you said you got?'

'Because I couldn't have got a degree without my A Levels or done my A Levels without my GCSEs. And, anyway, what am I going to do about the grades I don't list on my CV?'

He paled. 'What did you say?'

'Well, I don't put my C in General Studies on my CV. It was like a joke A Level they just told us to do to see if you got a good grade. If you didn't, then our teachers said we could just leave it off our CV.'

'But if they asked for your exam results, not including one of them is illegal.'

'Oh come on,' I said. 'What, are they going to arrest me?'

'Yes,' he said. 'It's breaking the law.'

'Huh,' I said, thinking of the myriad far more extreme embellishments my British friends and colleagues had made to their CVs.

To be British in the presence of a German bureaucrat is like being a rhino shipped over to the Tudor court for the amusement of the King. The fact that I don't have an ID card has been a particular source of wonder. 'But how does anyone know who you are?'

Awe-inspiring too was the fact that, when I didn't want to pay 'Church Tax', I could not prove that I was not a member of the Church of England because I didn't have a form from the church saying that I had left.

'But what church were you a member of, then?' the woman in the tax office asked me.

'I wasn't a member of any church. You don't become a member of a church in England. You just go.'

'"You just go",' she said, laughing, and then waited patiently for me to say something that wasn't a joke.

When Tom and I were finally able to register our UK marriage in Berlin, the woman at the registry office slowly took our English wedding certificate from the envelope and lifted it like someone who had just found some foreign underpants in their husband's car. 'It has handwriting on it,' she said breathlessly, holding it by the corners.

'They handwrite wedding certificates in England,' I said.

'Frau Weigt,' she called, unfolding it to its full foolscap length. 'An English wedding certificate.'

Her colleague shrieked.

'I will make a copy,' the bewildered woman said. '*Mein Gott!*' came her gleeful cry from the next-door room a few seconds later. 'Frau Weigt! It doesn't even fit in the photocopier!'


## Nine Months

Before we began our application meetings, which would take place once a month for, appropriately, nine months, we were asked to write a thousand words on our personal histories. In this written history, we were encouraged to reflect on our childhoods, how we were parented, how we would like to parent, what school life was like, what we found challenging, why we wanted children.

Alongside our application meetings, we were asked to attend a weekly adoption course that would help prepare us for the application process and the adoption. On this course the thousand-word personal history had been talked about in hushed tones. But, for a writer and a psychotherapist, it not only seemed relevant, but also fascinating.

'I don't have that many questions on your backgrounds,' Frau Schwenk said, leafing through our reports at our first meeting. 'Your texts were ... well, they were quite detailed.'

'Yes,' we said.

'No stone left unturned.'

'No,' we said.

Many people on our adoption course found these meetings intrusive. Tom and I were generally delighted.

'In the next two meetings each of you will individually have an hour to talk about your childhood.'

'An hour?' I said, my eyes sparkling. 'To talk about myself.'

'I'm afraid so,' our social worker said.

Tom swallowed. 'Who gets to go first?'

It struck me often during the application process that a nine-month exploratory course before conception would in fact be invaluable for anyone considering having a child. We were asked to reflect on what was good about our own childhoods and what was bad. We were confronted with the realities of the different reasons children might be adopted, all of which raised complex issues that would have to be dealt with as our prospective child grew up.

We felt, as most parents do, I'm sure, that we would be open, empathetic and honest with our child whatever their history. But time and time again our social worker gently pointed out that honesty alone is not a panacea.

'How would you talk to your child about their mother's background?'

'We would talk about her as much as they wanted. Be completely open about that history. You know, so it didn't become something that was like this secret that we suddenly revealed to them when they were eighteen. That would be terrible.'

'And with friends and family?'

'Also completely open.'

'OK. But – to take an example – we have a number of children whose mothers worked as prostitutes and that's how they were conceived. How would you talk about that if that was the case for your child?'

'Just be honest, I suppose.'

'But what about a scenario in which, say, your niece and nephew know that your son or daughter's biological mother was a prostitute and they say something about it to your child when they're three or four.'

'OK. Maybe we wouldn't tell everyone about that. Just our child.'

'But how would you explain to a three-year-old what a prostitute does?'

Our social worker didn't mean this rhetorically. The question was genuine.

'What's important,' she said after we had struggled to cobble together a reply, 'is that, as much as possible, your child learns about their story in a safe space created by you. And that means you sometimes need to think carefully about what you reveal and what you don't.'

Many applicants do not make it through the adoption process. But contrary to what had been our initial fears, it is rarely because they get through the meetings and then don't get rubber-stamped. The decision is nearly always on the side of the applicant parents who find, when encouraged to reflect on the realities of adoption, that they want to pause the process.

There is nothing wrong with this, you learn. The job of the adoption department is to make it completely clear to you what the realities of parenting and adopting are so that you can make an informed decision about whether it is something you really want to do.

The great advantage you have when you are adopting as a gay couple is that, most of the time – and certainly for us – it is firmly your plan A. If you have applied to adopt it is usually because you think it is the best way for you to start a family. And this means that, generally speaking, you are pretty open to the potential difficulties you might face parenting a child who has been adopted.

There are, of course, a lot of straight couples for whom this is also the case. But for many other straight couples prospective adoption represents the last stop on a long and, for some, painful journey.

This is exacerbated by the fact that there is an increasingly large array of options for couples who cannot naturally conceive, be it hormone therapies, IVF or egg and sperm donations. For countless people, including many couples in my own extended family, advances in assisted conception have led to families being created that would never have existed, which is a joyous thing. But it also means that the point at which a couple is able to firmly say they are not going to be able to have biological children of their own comes increasingly late. They have often not exhausted all other options until their mid-forties.

In Germany this leaves you very little wriggle room if you choose to adopt. Most countries require there to be a 'natural' gap between the adoptive parent and their child, which usually means an upper limit of forty years between your age and that of the child you're adopting. But because nearly all adoptions in Germany are of babies, this means that forty is generally the upper limit for adoption full stop.

There were a number of couples on our adoption course who

were dancing around this age limit and were clearly trying to make sense of what it might mean to adopt instead of conceive. We heard, often, a great desire in these parents for a child like any other; for a child like the child they had been dreaming of for the last twenty years. A child from a biological mother 'who didn't have any problems'.

I felt no sense of smugness when I listened to these parents' worried questions about the backgrounds of children in need of adoption. Gay parents looking to adopt are not innately better prepared to handle adoption. But for many of the straight couples, the adoption process was forcing them to confront the reality that the family they were going to create through adoption was going to be unlike the fantasy they had been gifted by the books they'd read and the films they'd watched, and which they'd been carrying around with them for almost four decades.

My husband and I had gone through exactly the same process of recognising that we were never going to have a family like the families we saw on TV. We'd just been forced to do it when we were fourteen.

## The Menu

For us, the part of the adoption process that was actually most difficult was putting together the profile for our prospective child.

'What about a child with a disability?' Frau Schwenk said, her ballpoint hovering over her clipboard.

'Probably not if it was very severe. Or a very severe intellectual disability.'

'It's likely to be quite a young child. So we won't know, of course, if it has an intellectual disability.'

'No. We would be fine if it turns out that they have a disability. But maybe we wouldn't start with that, if that makes sense. Is that OK?'

'There's no OK or not OK. It's vital that you're really honest about it, even if it feels quite cold. The worst thing that can happen is that you say yes to something that you're unsure about and then you can't cope when the child arrives. More adoptions break down than you think and it is always because the adoptive parent feels overwhelmed – it's vital that you're clear about what you can cope with.'

'OK. Then I think we'd say no to a serious physical or intellectual disability, but it's fine if it turns out later on that the child has a disability.'

'OK. What about if they were missing a foot?'

'A foot?'

'Yes. What if they didn't have a foot?'

'I mean . . . I suppose that would be OK.'

'Missing limbs?'

'Well, we live on the fourth floor. And we don't have a lift. So a wheelchair would be difficult. But no arms would be OK. I mean, that sounds really weird. I just mean—'

'There's no "really weird" here. We'll just make a list and let's see where we get. Try not to judge it.' She wrote something on her piece of paper and turned to a new sheet. 'Blind? Or deaf?'

'Yes,' I said.

'Really?' said my husband.

'Maybe. I don't know. I mean, if they had a hearing impairment or a visual impairment that would be OK, no?'

'Yeah, I suppose,' my husband said.

There was a pause. 'Let's lean towards no if you're unsure; you can always change it later.' She scribbled a note at the side of her list. 'What about the mother being a drinker?'

'If she was a severe alcoholic and had drunk through the pregnancy, then maybe not.'

'What if she'd had a few drinks? A couple of Baileys here or there at the weekend?'

'Would that have an effect?'

'We don't really know. Any amount of alcohol could theoretically have an effect.'

'I mean ... A couple of drinks would be fine, I think. Just not lots of drinks.'

'OK. What about ethnicity?'

## Migration Background

What Frau Schwenk actually asked was '*Und Migrationshintergrund?*', which literally means 'And their migration background?' This is the currently acceptable German term for what English speakers might currently refer to as BAME, global majority, BIPOC or 'person of colour'.

On the face of it, the term seems relatively technical and, as such, very German. Simply a description of a reality rather than an inaccurate description of someone's skin colour. It is far rarer in Germany to describe someone by the colour of their skin; the term *weiß* (white) is rarely used, for instance. Definitions are nearly always based on the perceived country of someone's origin.

Of course, 'migration background' is pretty dodgy in any technical sense, because words such as 'migrant' and 'migration' imply easily defined categories that are anything but. The most obvious question it raises is, migrated when? It is meant to be the primary definition of ethnic minority status in a country, but it assumes that the ethnic majority never migrated. By this definition, 97 per cent of Americans and 96 per cent of Australians would have a 'migration background'. And Germany is replete with ethnic minorities, from Jews to Muslims, who lived in Germany long before it was established as a nation state at the end of the nineteenth century. In its official definition, they would not be counted as having a 'migration background'.

This would be a problem if Germans attempted to use the term *Migrationshintergrund* in any kind of technical sense, which in fact they don't. 'Did they have a migration background,' a German is likely to say, 'or were they German?'

Hyphenated identities, like Turkish-German or Vietnamese-German, are grammatically correct, but rarely used. 'Turkish' or 'Arab' generally covers anyone who looks like they might be from North Africa, the Indian subcontinent or the Arabian Peninsula. 'Asian' covers anyone from South-East Asia. Although the term *weiß* is rarely used, *schwarz* is colloquially used for black people, but rarely uttered in the media or in political contexts.

Although issues of identity in countries like Britain or Ireland are deeply complex and regularly contested, the debate is nevertheless easier to frame in island nations as a question of who is allowed in or not. It is thus feasible for someone like Priti Patel to be both a second-generation migrant to Britain and a vocal supporter of Brexit on the basis that immigration is threatening class sizes.[1]

In Germany, though, the very notion of the nation state is an ethnic one. Before Germany existed as a country, 'Germans' were referred to as a people with their own language and their own culture and the establishment of Germany in 1871 was an attempt to establish a great nation state based along ethnic lines. Indeed, the current German constitution, the *Grundgesetz*, still refers to '*deutsche Volkszugehörigkeit*' or German ethnicity.[2]

In Germany, there continues to be a fundamental question about the meaning of 'non-German' citizens. It is still very common to refer to non-white Germans as *Ausländer* (foreigners). German newspapers continue to ask to what extent Germany is a *'Migrationsland'*, as if there were countries to which no one migrated. To be clear, in a country in which a quarter of the population have a *Migrationshintergrund* there is still a public discussion premised on the idea that the rest of Germany might somehow still be able to decide whether or not new arrivals to Germany can really be considered German.

As a British person in Germany, this relationship to race and ethnicity touches me in odd ways. When I filled out a grant application for non-German writers in Berlin, there was a tick box that read: 'Do you have a migration background?' I left it unticked because, from the way that I had heard it being used in conversation, on TV and in the newspapers, I understood 'migration background' to be synonymous with 'person of colour'. I understood the purpose of the box to be a way of making sure that underrepresented writers were being included in the grants being awarded. But then I spotted that they had added the official description of 'migration background'. It read: 'Were you or one or both of your parents born outside Germany?' And of course I and both my parents were born in England.

This struck me as a problem. On the one hand, in Germany I am without doubt an immigrant. And I am acutely aware of the racism inherent in our ongoing description of English people in Europe as 'ex-pats', white people in South Africa as 'white South Africans', but fourth-generation black people in the UK as 'immigrants'. But I was also aware of the possibility that ticking the box might mean that I was taking the place of someone who was genuinely underrepresented and marginalised in Germany because of their ethnic identity.

There is no doubt, by the way, that I am not marginalised for being English. And the reason is that I'm white and not Eastern European. Tabloids in Germany regularly decry the scores of school children in Germany who don't speak German at home. But whenever anyone hears me talking English to my son they cluck and say, 'Oh, how lucky for him, being brought up bilingual.'

Another common conversation goes something like this:

'Which primary school is Theo going to go to?'

'We don't know yet. We'll probably try and send him to the bilingual state school in Wilmersdorf, but we're in the catchment area for the Trebin School. It's the other side of the park, so we'd be able to walk there, which would obviously be lovely.'

'The Trebin School? Yeah, it's OK. It's getting better. A lot of foreigners go there, but the numbers are going down.'

'Well, I'm a foreigner, so . . .'

Laughter. 'You know what I mean, though. A proper foreigner.'

In this landscape, the question of whether or not parents with one ethnic background should be able to adopt children with a different ethnic identity is not a topic much debated in Germany. The question about your prospective child's 'migration background' is solely a question about your preferences as an adoptive parent.

Because, in Germany, most adopted children have to be given up for adoption by their parents rather than be removed by the courts, the parents – usually the mother – are asked whether they would like the child to be raised in a particular cultural or religious environment. On that basis, we said that if the mother was fine with us adopting their baby, then we would be fine with it too.

'Although,' I said, 'would that put us at a disadvantage? I

mean, aren't there going to be lots of mothers who aren't going to want their children to be raised by two dads?'

'Not in my experience,' our social worker said. 'A lot of the mothers like it; the idea that they'll still be their child's only mother, even if they're not around.'

## The Pool

We completed the adoption meetings. We had a check-up by a court-appointed doctor. We submitted three years of tax returns. We gathered countless personal documents, had others officially translated. Tom's parents travelled seven hours from Bonn to Berlin to be interviewed. We completed a weekly adoption evening class. And finally we were accepted into what the adoption team called 'the pool' in summer 2018.

There is no hierarchy in the pool, you are simply matched to a child if you best fit the child's needs. The average wait in the pool is one to two years. For some parents, the social worker already has a child in mind before the process is over; for other parents the call comes after five years. A substantial group of parents will never get a call.

It is an odd time. You are told that you shouldn't make any preparations for the arrival of the child, in case you are never matched. But you are also told only to go on holiday to places that you can get back from within twenty-four hours. We met a couple who had got the call in the middle of their holiday. They flew straight back from Spain only to be told in the taxi from the airport that the child's mother had changed her mind; she wouldn't be putting her child up for adoption.

We were lucky. Our wait was only three months.

# 5

# The Education Minister

## No Minister

Three weeks after we'd brought Theo home, Tom went back to work part time and for three days a week I was on my own with my son. They were exhausting, magical days.

Theo was still on a four-hour feeding rhythm. Drunk on milk, he'd collapse into sleep after every meal, knocked out enough that I could place him in his day bed for a precious hour during which I'd perform a farcical dumb show, running about the house in silence showering, peeing, stuffing the washing machine, standing in front of the fridge feeding from a buffet of sliced cheese from the packet, yoghurt from the pot and hunks of snapped-off cucumber, staring at the white flecks of sick-up that dappled the floor like bird shit, recalling benignly that I'd told myself the day before and the day before that that I needed to clean them up.

When I heard Theo cry I would race back to the living room and pull him onto my chest – the only place he would sleep for the remaining three hours until the next feed. Like a Manhattan socialite struck down in an opioid-and-vodka-fuelled malaise, I would sprawl on the sofa in my dressing gown with the phone, the computer, a glass of water, the remote controls to hand so that I could manage the rest of my life without moving an inch.

It was late November; the Berlin days had shrunk to seven hours of iron-grey light, occasionally peppered with a little sparkling snow. Theo was asleep with his plump cheek on my chest, intermittently sucking on the bright blue dummy he'd been given at the hospital that seemed to cover most of his face. I was watching TV with my nose in the blond velvet of his head and turned over to N-TV, a rolling German news channel, to watch the on-the-hour bulletin, which was followed by an interview with the new German Minister of Education, Anja Karliczek.

Concerned that Brexit was going to cause us issues with our adoption, I had applied for German citizenship the previous summer and had just been awarded dual citizenship, becoming officially British-German. I was struck for the first time, watching Karliczek speak, that she was my Education Minister now, responsible for my child's schooling. Until then, my feelings about German politics were like my feelings about sport: diverting, but not essential. I know who José Mourinho is, but I don't care if he gets sacked.

It was meant to be a get-to-know-the-new-minister interview and Karliczek came across well. Tall, loosely coiffed, bespectacled, she looked like the head of a Swiss bank. Walking through a decommissioned power plant in her home state of North-Rhine Westphalia with the interviewer, Louis Klamroth, she talked about her background and her views on education.

Then, seated beside a monumental industrial control panel from the 1960s, Klamroth asked her to comment on her criticisms of the way same-sex marriage had been voted through parliament in Germany in 2017 – she voted against – which opened the way for same-sex couples, like Tom and me, to adopt.

She had said back then, 'Contrary to what is always being claimed, there are no long-term studies on the effects on children of being brought up by same-sex couples. I believe that it is important for children's development that they experience the back-and-forth between mother and father.'*

Freshly promoted to Merkel's fourth cabinet, the new Education Minister did not gloss over her previous comments when the interviewer presented them to her afresh, but decided to double-down. She claimed again that there were no long-term studies on the effects on children of being brought up in what Germans rather charmingly refer to as 'rainbow families' (*Regenbogenfamilien*).

Karliczek struggled when Klamroth asked whether she thought that children with same-sex parents were less well brought up or less happy than other children. 'It's not about "happy" or "well brought up",' she said (God forbid!), 'it's fundamentally about something different. I am completely convinced that the majority of children who grow up in families in which they are wanted are well looked after and well brought up.'

Hardly a rock-hard foundation for a research proposal. What, then, did she see as the problem with having same-sex parents? 'As long as children are discriminated against in school or bullied, we will have a problem,' was her answer.[1]

This would imply, of course, that anything about a child's upbringing that could cause them to be bullied – from the

---

* What Karliczek actually said was: '*Im Gegensatz dazu, wie immer behauptet wird, gibt es keine Langzeitstudien zu den Auswirkungen auf Kinder in gleichgeschlechtlichen Partnerschaften. Meiner Einschätzung nach ist es für die Entwicklung von Kindern wichtig, das emotionale Spannungsfeld zwischen Vater und Mutter zu erleben.*' My translation is generous. What she literally said was that there is no research on the effects on children in same-sex partnerships. If she did mean that literally then she might be right, but I'm giving her the benefit of the doubt. She also talked about children experiencing the emotional *Spannungsfeld* between mother and father, which can be interpreted as 'back-and-forth' but literally means the 'field of tension between father and mother'. Something our poor angel will be missing out on.

colour of their skin to the relative wealth of their parents – is the problem of the parent and not the bully. Nevertheless, for Karliczek, this was enough of a reason to say that, until there is more research on the effects of having same-sex parents, parliament should not have brought in same-sex marriage and should have continued to block same-sex couples, like my husband and me, from adopting.

## Bullies

Beyond having no evidence to back up her claim that the children of same-sex parents are bullied more often than kids in other families,[2] Karliczek's focus on the reasons for bullying – and let's remember we're talking about the Education Minister here – cements the idea that there are reasons for getting bullied in the first place. It is premised on the notion that bullying exists as some external force outside human control, like a virus, and that having gay parents makes you more vulnerable to attack. Karliczek's solution – to stop the kids of same-sex parents getting bullied by stopping gay people from adopting – is rather like trying to stamp out carjacking by banning people from buying cars.

I say this to anyone who has ever been bullied in any context: there is only one reason that you were bullied and that is because your bully chose to bully you.

I was vigorously bullied in school. The 'reasons' I was bullied were threefold: I was a swot, I was suspected (correctly) of being gay, and I was a bit of a posho. The problem is that all of the qualities that marked me out as a potential victim were found in abundance in countless other students who were left alone. My friend Simon was cleverer than me in every class we were in, became head boy, and was never bullied for being a swot.

My friend Alan was exquisitely camp, wrote queer *Star Trek* parodies, and was never bullied for being gay. My friend James had a pool, a paddock for a pony and a two-acre garden, and was never bullied for being posh.

If there aren't any reasons for being bullied, then why was I bullied when those other boys were not? It's true that I did not cut a very physically intimidating figure in school and I had little interest in sport; in other words, to those boys stronger than me I looked like I might lose in a fight. But I was of average height, was not especially weedy. There were other boys smaller and less physically fit than me who were not bullied.

Part of the problem was certainly that I didn't try to fit in. Although I lay in bed at night dreaming of being average, I also remember walking the polished lino of the school's corridors realising that I was never going to be an average schoolboy, so I shouldn't bother trying.

When we went to school, my brother and sister and I all had our parents' BBC accents, honed in their respective boarding schools. But as the year went on, my siblings' RP stylings gradually shifted to match the accents of their friends. This is what normally happens – children adapt how they speak to match their peer group rather than their parents. But my accent remained unchanged. And I remember, again quite consciously, feeling that I should keep the accent of home, where I was safe and accepted, rather than the accent of school, where I was not.*

---

* This is the best explanation I have for why I speak the way I speak. But recently I listened to separate interviews with the gay comedian Tom Allen and the gay writer and barrister Mohsin Zaidi. They both talked about being educated at state schools and ending up with accents much posher than those of their school friends. It made me wonder if there is something else more complex going on here that I don't yet understand. Were our BBC accents an attempt to create some social capital in an environment where we had none? Were we subconsciously attempting to separate ourselves from our peers? Did we reject the accent of our bullies? Neither Allen nor Zaidi could put their finger on why they had ended up speaking the way they do and I struggle to do the same. I'll let you know if we work it out.

And while I knew it was vital that I kept my sexuality hidden, I often made Carry On-style jokes, had a running gag with another friend that we were lovers, read *Maurice* on the school bus and, for 'Tarts and Vicars' day during our school's charity week, invariably came dressed up as a tart and always managed to source size-ten stilettos to do it in.

None of these are reasons for my being bullied, though. You might say that it was not surprising that I was bullied, but the suggestion that the source of my bullying is to be found in me is galling. I did not deserve to be bullied. No one deserves to be bullied. Bullying is not inevitable and there are countless things that education ministers can do to tackle it. Blaming the parents of the victims of bullying is not one of them.

## A Glance at the Research

The most obvious problem with Karliczek's arguments is that there have in fact been many studies on the effects of having same-sex parents, many of them long-term, and the research is ongoing. Just this year, a study of over 3,000 same-sex parents in the Netherlands – where same-sex marriage has been legal for twenty years – showed that 'children raised by same-sex parents are likely to perform at least as well as (if not better than) children raised by different-sex parents in school'.[3]

In Germany, a 2009 study commissioned by the Bavarian Justice Department and led by the University of Bamberg focused on over a thousand children with same-sex parents and found that 'the wellbeing of a child is not connected with the sexual orientation of the parents, but rather the quality of their upbringing and the climate in the family'.[4] Go figure!

There have even been studies on the specific question of whether the children of same-sex parents are in fact bullied more. US studies have shown that only about 8 per cent of children with same-sex parents are bullied because they have same-sex parents. But those studies also make the consequences of that bullying clear: the 8 per cent of children who were bullied had more behavioural and psychological problems than the 92 per cent of children who were not.[5]

For most children of gay and lesbian parents, their unique upbringing is actually something that they actively value. The vast majority of these children report feeling positive about being the children of same-sex parents and believe that it allows them to be more open to and empathetic with others. And, when asked, the major problem that they faced was not bullying, but unintentionally insensitive remarks from their peers related to having same-sex parents.[6] Exactly the sort of remarks that Karliczek's comments fuel.

A number of studies have suggested that the children of same-sex parents have slightly better educational and psychological outcomes than kids brought up by straight parents, with an Italian study showing the children of gay fathers coming out best.[7] The researchers suggest that the advantage has nothing to do with gay fathers being innately better parents than lesbian mothers or straight parents, it is simply that the harder it is to get a child, the more wanted the child is likely to be. And isn't there in fact something very beautiful in this? The depth of one's desire to have a child makes one a better parent.

Straight couples who don't want children can still have children by mistake, and even more have children they feel ambivalent about having, in relationships they feel ambivalent about being in. For gay men, there is almost no quick fix. Whether it's a casual arrangement, surrogacy, foster care or adoption, gay fathers don't become parents without a substantial commitment of time and effort and money* over years rather than months. And the money means that the children of same-sex parents tend to be brought up in higher socioeconomic environments, which explains most, but not all, of the advantage that the children of same-sex parents have in school.[8]

In the face of no anecdotal or empirical data suggesting that children are negatively affected by having same-sex parents, Karliczek must, then, have been able to name something pretty concrete about the psychological disadvantages of having two fathers or two mothers (or, for that matter, one mother, one father or no parents). She did. She said that it was important that children experience how men and women deal with competition differently.

For someone who has fought their way to the top of government, it seems odd at best for Karliczek to suggest that men and women's relationship to competition is so innately different that children with same-sex parents will be so dangerously skewed to one approach to competition that it would be better for them never to have been adopted at all. How does she conceive of this playing out, I wonder? Gay fathers breeding a generation of Donald Trumps and Margaret Thatchers, perhaps, ruling over the indolent spawn of lesbian mothers whose children never had the energy to get out of bed?

More to the point, being blessed with both a mother and a father did not mean that Karliczek's children had a perfect

---

* Money changes hands in surrogacy although many countries only allow you to cover the expenses of the surrogate mother; generally you cannot pay her to carry your baby. Foster carers in most countries also receive government support. You receive no financial support when you adopt in Germany or the UK, even during the initial stage when you are legally your child's foster carer. But adoption still has a financial impact, because there are a range of financial requirements one must fulfil to adopt. You have to have a home with a spare room, for instance, and you have to be able to prove that you are financially stable.

balance of male and female perspectives in their upbringing, because, like all children in the West, they will have been raised almost exclusively by women.

In the UK, working fathers spend seven times as much time with their children as they did fifty years ago, meaning that your modern British working dad spends an exhausting thirty-five minutes a day with his child.[9] In Germany, as in the US,[10] fathers spend an average of one hour a day with their children – an average that includes the weekend. That's quadrupled over the past fifty years, but it's still ... well, an hour a day. By the time they're eighteen, then, your average German *Kind* has spent 6,570 hours with their *Papa*.* By sharing childcare, Tom and I hit 6,570 hours by the time Theo turned two; the average German *Mama* has already overtaken her husband for good by the time their child is eighteen months old.

So Karliczek is absolutely right that, aged two, our son had had far less contact with responsible adult females than most children have had. But then he went to nursery and embarked upon what will likely be two decades of female care and instruction. In German nurseries, 95.4 per cent of nursery teachers are women.[11] In primary school women represent 87 per cent of teaching staff, and in secondary school 66 per cent of teachers are female. And the education system is rapidly feminising: 73 per cent of secondary school teachers under thirty are women and, if Theo decides to go to university,† 80 per cent of his fellow students will be female.[12] These figures are mirrored in developed countries across the world.

By the time we take our son off for his first day at primary school he will have evened out the masculine imbalance of his childhood and, from that day forth, he will be living in an

---

* Frau Karliczek's husband's a pilot, a fifty-hour-a-week job, so we're being generous in our assumptions here.
† No pressure, love.

increasingly female world. Even as a boy with two dads, Theo will have spent far more time being educated, brought up and cared for by women than men by the time he leaves school.[13]

We don't, of course, need studies into same-sex parenting to challenge Karliczek's claim that gay people should not be allowed to adopt on the basis that a child needs a mother and a father. If she was actually driven by a desire to make sure that children are brought up by a parent of each sex, she would be coming up with policies to address the 2 million children being brought up in Germany by a single parent, rather than the handful of gay men and women adopting each year.[14] And as to her claim that children who are not brought up by both a man and a woman might have an issue dealing with competition, we might ask any Barack Obama, Michael Phelps, Adele, Oprah Winfrey or Tom Hanks about how being brought up by a single parent affected their drive.

Finally, what the statistics make very clear is that, aside from bullying, the only other factor that has a visceral effect on the outcomes of children of same-sex couples is how positive or negative the legal environment in their country is towards same-sex parenting.[15] That is to say, the only guaranteed way that Karliczek could make life better for the children of same-sex parents would be to stop challenging the rights of their families.


## Science as a Tool for Prejudice

Even if you agree broadly with my arguments here, there may be a little voice in your head, a niggling doubt, along the lines of, 'But if Karliczek is just suggesting doing a neutral scientific study about the effects of having same-sex parents, what would be the problem of doing it? If you're sure there's no issue with gay parenting, why would you be bothered about someone doing more research on it? In the end, isn't it just going to prove you right?'

You'd be correct. Based on the lashings of data already available on same-sex parenting, there's little question that any study Karliczek might be suggesting would show that children in same-sex relationships do just as well, if not better, than children being brought up by straight couples. At the same time, the mere suggestion that this research remains necessary is, in itself, a political tactic that subtly suggests there is something amiss, something worth investigating. And this follows on from a grand tradition of science being used as a tool to attack minority groups.

Still not convinced? Well, imagine that I was working in Anja Karliczek's Department of Education and I came up with the idea of doing a study on whether menstruation affects female headteachers' ability to make executive decisions. Frau Karliczek would, I suspect, fire me. And quite rightly. But – I could argue at my inevitable tribunal – we know that women's moods are affected by menstruation. And if you believe hormones don't affect women's decision-making skills, why are you worried about the research?

The response would be two-fold. For a start, we don't just research anything that comes into our heads. We observe something happening, we come up with a hypothesis of what could be going on and then we test that hypothesis. Edward Jenner often heard the local legend that milk-maids didn't die from smallpox; he guessed it probably had something to do with the fact that they all caught cowpox, and he tested that hypothesis to help create the world's first modern vaccine.* He

---

* The root of the word 'vaccine' is Jenner's Latin name for cowpox 'Variolae vaccinae' (literally 'smallpox of the cow'). Although Jenner was the first person to come up with the idea of inoculating people against smallpox with the related but less deadly cowpox, there are records of successful inoculations against smallpox using smallpox itself in India, Africa and China centuries before the practice was observed in the Ottoman Empire in the eighteenth century.

didn't just see a pocked cow and think, Oh, I wonder what would happen if I stuck a bit of that pus in someone's arm. Maybe it'll cure smallpox.

There is also a giant pragmatic hole behind all of these political feelings dressed up as science in that the imagined results, even if they backed up the claims these politicians are making, would in fact have no practical meaning. If we take Karliczek's research proposal, what purpose would it actually serve? She is talking specifically about stopping same-sex parents adopting, because she believes – on a hunch – that a study might show that the children of same-sex parents might, on average, have slightly worse outcomes than the children of straight parents.

So let's say that she discovered that the children of same-sex parents received, on average, one less GCSE than the children of straight parents. Would that mean that same-sex parents should not be able to adopt children? Of course it wouldn't. Because adoption agencies are not assessing an average parent, they are assessing real people. If they are trying to place a child with serious learning difficulties and they are choosing between straight parents who are full-time bankers and a lesbian couple who both work part time as teachers for kids with special needs, then average school results are meaningless.

Saying that we need more research on same-sex parenting before we should allow same-sex couples to adopt is saying that you believe that the effects of same-sex parents adopting is so damaging that it trumps every other consideration when placing a child for adoption. I think even the German Education Minister could not claim that that was the case.

Of course, as we've already seen, the extensive research we have actually shows that children brought up by same-sex couples have slightly better outcomes, both psychologically and educationally. So we could reword the findings of the existing research to say that the children of straight parents have slightly worse academic outcomes than children with same-sex parents. Does that mean that we should ban straight parents from adopting children? Of course not. But not just because that would be politically and practically absurd, but also because it is a misunderstanding of the meaning of the statistics. A small statistical difference between two groups gives us almost no practical information about individuals in that group. The statistical fact that, in tennis, men can, on average, serve faster than women does not mean that, being a man, I can serve faster than Serena Williams.

Perhaps the best answer I can give you as to whether Karliczek's call for more research on the long-term effects of having same-sex parents was a political one is that, over four years later, there is no sign of any study. She has not changed her position – a position warmly welcomed by her core voters – but she has also not enacted a research project that she apparently believes is so essential we should stop same-sex couples adopting children until it is complete.[16]

## Always Here

Karliczek's take on same-sex parenthood also illustrates a classic rhetorical trick used by politicians attacking something for political purposes: speaking about a situation that you cannot fundamentally change in a way that implies that you, and in turn the voter, could. This turns something complex about how we might allow people to deal with a multifaceted social situation in the real world into an apparently black-and-white decision.

It's an effective trick, because it's so appealing. Who wants to hear from their MP that they've lost their job due to a

complex set of global movements and national economic decisions that has made the country as a whole more wealthy but
disadvantaged a number of groups, communities and industries in particular areas, including the one that was dominant
in your town when your parents moved there, which is unfair,
but it was factored into the calculations, so you can't really do
anything about it, unless you want to retrain, but you're too
old for that, so you're just one of the people that missed out?
'Immigrants took your job' sounds much better. You're happy
because you have someone to blame, and your MP's happy
because you're not blaming her.

Karliczek employs this rhetorical stratagem by talking
about same-sex parenting as if she, the German Bundestag or
German voters could do anything to stop it. It is of course the
case that Karliczek and her parliamentary colleagues could
make things harder for same-sex parents – and indeed her
comments do exactly that – but she does not have the power
to decide whether or not same-sex parents exist.

The introduction of same-sex marriage in Germany made it
easier for people in same-sex relationships to adopt, because,
in Germany, being married is generally a prerequisite for
adoption. However, as we've already discussed, compared to
the UK, adoption is much harder in Germany, with only about
800 children being adopted each year.[17] Because of the data
protection and privacy laws around adoption, there is no hard
data on how many adoptions since 2017 have been to same-sex
parents, but even if queer adopters were adopting at the same
rate as straight people – and, anecdotally, we have only met
three other same-sex couples during the whole adoption process, so that seems very unlikely – the families that Karliczek
is talking about disenfranchising make up about 0.4 per cent of
the 9,500 families in Germany headed by same-sex parents.[18]
In other words, Karliczek is happy to make life very difficult for

the forty or so same-sex parents a year who might be adopting in Germany, in order to score a few points for her more conservative voters.

Same-sex parents and single people have been able to foster children in Germany for years, including becoming long-term foster carers, which is very similar to open adoptions in the USA and the UK. Just as in every other country in the world, there are far more children in the care system than there are parents to foster them. The number of children being taken into care is rising while the number of prospective parents for both fostering and adoption is dropping.[19] Local authorities across the Western world are, in fact, desperate for same-sex foster and adoptive parents, not least because they are far more likely to take on so-called 'hard-to-place' children who are being overlooked for adoption because they are in sibling groups, are older, have special needs or have minority ethnic backgrounds.[20]

But beyond the care system, 'rainbow families' have existed in Germany, and across the globe, for as long as families have existed. Even today, the most common reason for a child to be raised by same-sex parents is that the children were conceived when one or more of those parents were in a heterosexual, cis-gendered relationship.[21] Actor Cynthia Nixon is just such a parent, along with Kelly McGillis and Jan Morris. Anthony Perkins was such a parent, as was Danny Kaye and Oscar Wilde.

And good parents at that. Before his conviction and imprisonment for gross indecency, Wilde was a dedicated father, spending hours sailing and swimming with his boys, and reading them stories. In contrast to the authoritarian Victorian fathers of the age, his son Vyvyan described him as 'the smiling giant, always exquisitely dressed, who crawled about the nursery floor with us and lived in an aura of cigar smoke and Eau de Cologne'.[22]

The same is also true of the countless same-sex families that started out as opposite-sex families. Despite the fact that trans people are far more likely to become parents than cis-gendered gay and lesbian people,[23] media coverage of these families is minimal. When media outlets do write about trans parents – still often using luridly B-movie headlines, like 'The Pregnant Man'[24] – they focus on the hoops trans people have to jump through to have children, even when they are able to give birth to them themselves. These stories remain highly topical: just last year in the UK, the journalist Freddy McConnell lost his battle to be legally recognised as his child's father.[25] But one could get the impression – as is true of the way that trans issues are nearly always framed – that we are talking about a phenomenon of the last decade.

In fact, trans parents, like all queer parents, are nothing new. Thousands of children have been and continue to be parented by one or more trans men or women who started parenting before their transition. Studies show that trans parents are numerous and that they make great parents; being raised by someone who is trans has no effect on the happiness or wellbeing of children.[26]

Indeed, in those families in which a father became a mother or vice versa, the parent's transition can represent not a break from marriage and family life, but a commitment to it. As Jan Morris wrote in her 1974 account of her transition, she felt that, by transitioning, 'I had, so far as I could, honoured the responsibilities of my marriage; rather than go mad, or kill myself, or worst of all perhaps infect everyone around me with my profoundest melancholy.'[27] Her children were not traumatised by now having two mothers. 'The process was infinitely slow and subtle, and through it all anyway, as I hope they sensed, I remained the same affectionate self.'[28]

## How Hard-Won Rights Can Be Lost

I have talked a lot about facts in this chapter, but actually my overwhelming feeling, as I watched Anja Karliczek on that N-TV interview with my son on my chest, was not anger at her misguided opinions, but fear.

The Minister of Education in the country I lived in stood firmly for a policy that would have denied me my child. Before that moment I had worried about bigoted individuals saying hateful things to me, my husband and my son. But I had not worried about our rights being rolled back. Watching that interview, I felt the ground beneath my feet becoming a little less stable. When I wanted to feel most secure I felt genuinely afraid for my family; afraid of bringing up my son in a country in which senior politicians in the ruling party were questioning our family's right to exist.

It is impossible to live in Berlin and not be acutely aware that social progress is not an unstoppable stream. Every time I visit Schöneberg City Hall to drop off or collect some new document related to my or my son's right to travel, to work, to live in Berlin, I see little signs high up on the lampposts that mark the gradual removal of Jewish Germans' rights in the first half of the twentieth century. They remind me that the Nazis didn't just start rounding up Jews into concentration camps; it was a slow, progressive erosion of rights, the government constantly feeling out how far it could go.

Very far, as it turned out.

In 1933, just a few months after Hitler was elected, Jews were removed from university and government positions. A few weeks later they were banned from working as lawyers, judges, doctors and teachers. Two years later, in 1935, marriages between Jewish people and 'Aryan' Germans were forbidden and citizenship was removed for Jewish people, who became state subjects without any civil rights. Three years after that, in 1938, Jewish people were required to register their assets, their children were removed from German state schools, Jewish doctors were no longer allowed to treat non-Jewish patients, and their movements were restricted.[29]

In 1939 Nazi Germany invaded Poland, and just six years later, at the end of the Second World War, a community of 522,000 German Jews had been reduced to some 20,000.[30] Nazi Germany murdered, deported and forced out over 96 per cent of its Jewish population. The Nazis lost the war, but their aim of ridding the country of its Jewish community was an unqualified success.

Most of us know the bones of this story. What we often miss is that this complete eradication of a whole community was not a case of a white European country expelling an immigrant population. Jewish Germans were not recently arrived refugees. Jews began to settle in Germanic countries from AD 321, around the same time as the Anglo-Saxons were arriving in Britain. In the eighteenth century, after centuries of repression and violence, the Haskalah, or Jewish Enlightenment, led by the philosopher Moses Mendelssohn, allowed Jewish people in Germany to slowly gain their human rights. Civic equality for Jews was won in a number of German lands as early as 1782, and after the liberal revolutions of 1848 and then the foundation of Germany as a nation state in 1871, Jews achieved substantial legal equality.

When we talk about the darkest time in Germany's history, we often talk about what 'the Germans' did to 'the Jews'. We talk about these two groups as if they were separate people. But of course, between 1941 and 1945, the Germans were murdering their own. Over the course of twelve short years, Adolf Hitler, an Austrian immigrant who moved to Germany when he was fourteen, stripped away centuries of hard-won rights from a community that had been slowly integrating into the country for sixteen centuries. And then he had them murdered.

It is a stark reminder of how quickly integration can collapse. And in 2022, we can already see in many countries that the progress queer people have scraped together over the last centuries is being rolled back. From Croatia to California, Bermuda to Romania, governments have been putting forward referendums aimed at banning same-sex marriage, some of which have been successful.

Authoritarian governments in Uganda and Hungary, Kenya and Russia are weaponising opposition to LGBTQ+ people in countries that had previously turned a blind eye to same-sex relationships. In 2021 alone, thirteen new laws covering thirty-seven states were introduced in the USA that restrict the rights of trans people, banning them from being able to change their birth certificates and use bathrooms that match their gender, and stopping young trans people from participating in sports and gender-affirming healthcare.[31] And queer people's legal rights are even being attacked in countries like Poland and Turkey – countries in which there have *never* been laws banning same-sex sexual activity.

We cannot forget that the vast majority of the global population, and consequently the majority of queer people in the world, still live in countries in which their rights are substantially curtailed. In ten of these countries the most severe punishment for consensual sex between men is death.

Queer people represent the perfect social minority, and thus the perfect political scapegoat, because they consistently appear in every society, but don't reproduce. There will never be a country, even a city, with a gay majority; there will never be a gay homeland. When commentators refer to a 'black' city, like Detroit, they mean a city that is majority black. When they refer to a 'gay' city, like San Francisco, they mean a city that is 6 per cent gay. Women can be in a minority in the workforce and move towards parity,[32] but there has never been an industry, a city or corporation that was majority gay and there never will be.

As hard as we should strive for a perfectly equal society in which sexuality and gender are meaningless, I am also aware that we have an inbuilt instinct for identifying groups to which we do and do not belong. But my hope, when I met my husband back in 2006 and we talked about having kids, was that being gay in Britain or the USA could one day be like being Jewish in Britain or the USA. Finding out someone was gay, I thought, might one day be like finding out that Amy Winehouse or Harrison Ford or Rashida Jones were Jewish. You would say, 'Huh, I didn't know that.' And then you wouldn't really think about it again. It would be something that has meaning for the people in that group but would not be hugely meaningful to people outside that community, beyond benign curiosity.

With the re-emergence of populism across the world, with antisemitic abuse reaching a record high in Britain in 2021 and one in four American Jews experiencing antisemitism in the same time period, this comparison has sadly foundered.[33] And it sheds light on how easy it is, even in countries like Britain and America, for hard-fought-for rights to crumble away.

## A Defence of Lives

Before I began seriously to look into ways of making a family, my initial concern with the concept of surrogacy was the moment I would have to explain to my child where they came from. That I would have to tell them that the reason they didn't have a mother was down to a choice that I had made. My position softened – as these positions do – when I heard more stories from parents who had started their families with surrogates and had met their children. Did I actually see a vacuum in these children's lives? Or was I holding on to a well-meaning prejudice that didn't stand up to examination?

In 2017, a year before Tom and I adopted, my ex-boss at the Serpentine Gallery, Julia Peyton-Jones, made headlines when she became a new mother at sixty-four. Her decision was met with derision by many. Some commentators, like Ulrika Jonsson, described it as 'selfish and irresponsible'.[34]

In one way, I was also surprised by the news; Julia was already in her fifties when I started working for her in 2007. But in another way I was not. For better and for worse, she was never very interested in limits. 'Just make it happen, old bean,' she used to say to me over her reading glasses whenever I appeared at her office door to point out that we couldn't afford whatever the artist in question was demanding.

My initial reaction to the news, like the reaction of Julia's critics, was also to count forward to how old she would be when her daughter went to school, when she graduated, when she might get married. But then I was faced with the same question that I had faced with surrogacy. I thought about a friend of mine whose dad was in his sixties when he was born. I thought about my dad losing his father when he was eleven. I thought about my friend Lorna who died of cancer in her early forties leaving two young children behind. And the question I asked myself was: do I really think that the loss of a parent – even if that parent is implicated in that loss – is so terrible that the child in question would've been better off not being born? The answer, for me, was no.

I don't mean to say that there are no moral questions to consider in surrogacy, sperm or egg donation, in parents having families later and later in life, in who can and should adopt. I'm not arguing here for a natal free-for-all. But we need to respond to these concerns in a way that corresponds to their actual influence in these children's lives.

Like Karliczek and her misdirected concern about bullied children, our concern is often misdirected at people making decisions that challenge our assumptions about parenthood. But when you go through the adoption process, meet other adopters, talk to social workers in detail about real children who have experienced real trauma, you realise that it is in fact glaringly obvious what really fucks children up. It's poverty. It's sexual abuse, which nearly always takes place in the home. It's neglect. It's multiple homes and multiple care homes. We are very, very far away from solving these problems and we have whole libraries filled with studies that make it clear how damaging these things are.

People like Karliczek, like Dolce, like Jonsson obsessively point the finger at queer parents, at parents who use sperm donors and surrogates, at older parents. But if they really want to change children's lives for the better they should be directing their outrage towards the inequalities and conflicts that are genuinely and measurably destroying children's lives in our own countries and abroad at this very moment.

We are constantly telling anyone who doesn't fit a very narrow image of what it means to be a family that they are selfish for wanting children. We tell single mothers they are irresponsible for having children and that their kids will be damaged by missing out on a male role model. We tell the parents of only children that denying their children siblings is akin to neglect. We tell mothers who can't breastfeed that they are poisoning their babies.

What people like Anja Karliczek are telling gay people is that their children will be bullied and that it is their fault. That gay

marriage and gay parenting challenge and undermine the traditional family. But what I often imagine is some archaeologist
of the distant future cracking open our books, dusting off our
hard drives, and discovering that we created a society in which
the people who couldn't have children biologically looked after
the children of those who weren't able to care for their biological
children. Wouldn't that archaeologist think she was reading
about a utopia? If someone told you about the discovery of an
uncontacted society, deep in the jungle, in which no child was
neglected, where a child being loved and having a secure home
was more important to the community than the sex of who was
raising that child – wouldn't you think that was paradise?

The question we need to ask ourselves when we are about
to wag the finger is: are we putting as much or considera-
bly more time and effort into questioning and combating
the countless things that we know destroy children's lives?
Things like neglect. Things like sexual abuse. Things like
war and poverty. Things like bullying and the extraordinary
social pressures put on young people trying to form identities
in a digital age in which they are bombarded with images
of doctored and curated lives and bodies that are literally
unobtainable.

I would like to make the radical suggestion that all kids
are good kids; that there are no kids whose family set-up is so
peculiar that it would've been better that they had never been
born. I would like to invite Anja Karliczek and politicians
like her to take a completely dispassionate look at the societies
in which they wield so much power. And to commit, not to
trying to ban the types of people who are offering safe and
loving homes to the thousands of children in desperate need
of them, but to tackling the poverty, addiction and deprivation
that leads to those children having to be taken into care in the
first place.

## Emotions

Long before my husband and I brought our son home, I was walking over the snowy cobbles of Berlin with my friend Michael telling him that Tom and I were considering adoption. 'If you think about it,' I said, 'there are far more kids in need of a home than available parents. So even if you think that kids should have a mum and a dad, that's impossible for all kids. So it's obviously a good thing for same-sex couples to take up the slack. And if you think about it—'

'Ben,' he said, cutting me off, 'you don't need to justify it.'

In the moment, I was a bit offended. I thought he was wrong. I thought it was very important for me to build a defence for why it was OK for me and my husband to have children.

Now I see that he was pointing out that I was doing something that prospective straight parents almost never do: thinking deeply about whether they *should* have children.

When I find myself standing in the shower having these defensive arguments in my head, the shampoo having long since circled the plughole, or when I find myself feeling sick to my stomach with hopeless rage reading about some new atrocity being committed against a queer person in the name of tradition, of culture, of religion, it always makes me think about Toni Morrison's oft-quoted deconstruction of racism:

> The function, the very serious function of racism is distraction. It keeps you from doing your work. It keeps you explaining, over and over again, your reason for being. Somebody says you have no language and you spend twenty years proving that you do. Somebody says your head isn't shaped properly so you have scientists working on the fact that it is. Somebody says you have no art, so you dredge that up. Somebody says you have no kingdoms, so you dredge

that up. None of this is necessary. There will always be one more thing.[35]

In a sense, what I have done in this chapter is given in to exactly that distraction. If I gave this book to Anja Karliczek to read, she wouldn't change her mind. She is already convinced of her position and she would simply find another problem for me to scurry away and solve. The problem here is that I have used truths to try and combat prejudice, and prejudice has nothing to do with the truth.

The answer to Karliczek's argument, the faultless argument, is my son. When I find myself lost in building defence after defence for my life and my family, I watch Theo running off to find a book, climbing into bed to show us the cardboard fork-lift truck that I glued back into his pop-up vehicle encyclopaedia. I kiss the crown of his perfect head and know that, when all is said and done, a misguided politician doesn't matter. I know that he matters and that this family matters – perfect, like all families, in its imperfection.

# Closed Questions

## Brand New

Pushing our freshly bought pram out into a sheet-white November day for the first time, I felt conspicuous. The sheen of the pram's black polyester hood, its unmuddied wheels, Theo's spotless yellow blanket – all of it screamed: we're pretending to be parents. As we passed a group of mothers with their battered pushchairs and prams, their saliva-stained baby carriers and pockets blooming with tissues, grubby muslins* and half-sucked rice cakes, we felt that they could scent our new things, smell that we were trying too hard.

I kept fantasising that, before we got to the café, which we were cautiously pushing our baby towards, a police car was

---

* When you become a new parent in a bilingual relationship you have to learn a completely new vocabulary. I often struggle when talking to friends and family back in England about things going on in Theo's life, because I want to say *Kita* for nursery and *Schnulli* for dummy. This is particularly difficult if you speak German half the time, because it's such a descriptive language that it's nearly always easier to picture the German word. A muslin in German, for instance, is a *Spucktuch* – literally a 'spit cloth'. Tom too had to learn a new set of words in English – the language we still speak together at home – and spent the first week of Theo's life asking me why we never had enough Muslins in the house.

going to pull up with a screech. The police officer would get out and gently say, 'Do you even know how to look after a baby?' And we would break down and say, 'No! We don't! We have no idea what we're doing!'

There was no police car, though. The mothers didn't turn their heads. Only in the café when we asked for some water to heat up his milk did the waitress pause for a split second to take in the two of us with our baby, before saying, 'Yes, of course.'

In 2018, two dads was not a complete unknown in Germany. As touched upon in the previous chapter, same-sex parents have been able to foster for some years and, before they were supported by the law, same-sex couples and singles found countless creative ways to start families, from Danish sperm donations* and surrogacy in the USA to casual arrangements with friends of the opposite sex. And yet, same-sex parenting remains comparatively rare. Of Germany's 14 million families with dependent children, 9,500 are headed by a same-sex couple or a gay or lesbian single parent; that's 0.7 same-sex families per 1,000 families. In the United States the ratio is three times this, in the UK about double.[1] Two dads are also much rarer than two mums.[2] Reactions of surprised interest, even in liberal old Berlin, are, therefore, perhaps to be expected.

Whether or not such reactions are comprehensible, they still make me feel extremely self-conscious, even when they're friendly. When we first took a train to Tom's parents in the

---

* Denmark is the only country in the EU that still guarantees sperm donors' anonymity. In the rest of the EU, the sperm donor's right to anonymity is overridden by the child's right to know who their biological father is. Denmark has thus become a mecca for queer and straight women starting a family alone or with their female partner.

Rhineland, we shared the children's carriage* with two new mothers,† one of whom pointed to our son and said, 'Do you mind me asking how you got him?'

'We adopted him,' Tom said.

She seemed pleased with that answer and went on to tell us a story about lesbian friends who'd used a sperm donor to conceive. The details became a little vague as the story went on and it became clear that they were a couple she had met rather than a couple she was friendly with.

I don't mind talking about our son's adoption – if I did, I wouldn't be writing this book – but the question, asked without any context, often makes me uncomfortable. For a start, her enquiry made it clear to us that we were so noticeably other that she had stepped outside the bounds of normal social behaviour to ask us a personal question she would likely not have asked had we not been two dads.

We were sharing the carriage with another mother with whom she did not share a single word. She had not leant over to her and said, 'Do you mind me asking if you were able to conceive naturally? Or was it IVF? Did you have a C section? Can't you breastfeed or don't you want to?' I was quite fascinated about why she was feeding her three-month-old pretzels, but I wouldn't have dreamt of commenting on it.

A year or two later, when I was reading Rebecca Solnit's book on being a woman without a child, *The Mother of All Questions*, I realised that it wasn't being asked about Theo's adoption that I found uncomfortable. It was the intention behind the question.

---

* That's right – German intercity trains have a special carriage for young families with small children, which you can book for no extra fee. They're completely separate from the other carriages, there is extra room for your prams, extra plugs, you get a free extra seat for your extra stuff, and some of them come with a climbing frame. *Blüh' im Glanze dieses Glückes!*

† There were no other men in our carriage. These mothers were travelling alone and long-distance with their babies, something that Tom and I have not done once in over three years, because it would clearly be awful.

Solnit, reflecting on how often she is asked about why she never had children, says:

> Just because the question can be answered doesn't mean that anyone is obliged to answer it, or that it ought to be asked. [...] We talk about open questions, but there are closed questions, too, questions to which there is only one right answer, at least as far as the interrogator is concerned. These are questions that push you into the herd or nip at you for diverging from it, questions that contain their own answers and whose aim is enforcement and punishment.[3]

The problem with the woman's question was that it was not really about us. Like the many people who had asked Solnit why she hadn't had children, the question served a social function. The woman on the train did not seem to be particularly interested in our story. She was interested in showing us that she was comfortable with us. She was shoring up her own image of herself as the sort of person who was not bothered by gay parents. But like people who claim that they can't be racist because they just 'don't see colour', her show of charmed disinterest revealed the very opposite. She was keenly aware of our presence; much more so than the silent mother beside her who didn't give us a second glance.

I recognise this performance, because it is one I take part in all the time. The moment I hear the slightest twinge of an accent, I feel a rising anxious excitement in my belly. It's the same goody-two-shoes feeling I used to get in school when the teacher began to ask a question and I realised that I knew the answer. I knew that being right wouldn't make me popular, but I couldn't resist. 'Anyone else *other* than Ben,' the teacher would say, peering around the class hopefully.

The trouble, I have learned over the years, is that a person's nationality, a person's ethnicity, a person's sexuality or gender is inevitably the least interesting thing about them, because it's one of the few things about them that they played no part in choosing. Even if someone is from somewhere that you are deeply interested in, they are often the worst person to enthuse about it with, because it is at once extremely banal to them and yet filled with emotional ambivalence. Asking someone what they think about their country is like asking them what they think about their own face.

Any conversation one begins in reference to someone's homeland, sexuality or cultural heritage quickly dies to nothing. Because what does one really have to say about the unchangeable realities of one's life?

As a gay person, you still often get some version of, 'Oh, you're gay. My cousin's gay.'

'Oh,' you say. 'Cool.'

'He got married.'

'Oh right.'

'Are you married?'

'Uh-huh.' You tap the stem of your wine glass and stare out over the marquee.

I do the same the moment I hear a rhotic R.

'You're from Ireland?'

'Yes.'

'Whereabouts?'

'Wexford.'

'Oh, I love Ireland. I was in Kerry. Beautiful.'

'It is.'

Friendly smile. Nod. Silence.

'Rainy.'

'It is rainy.'

Silence.

*

Although it has a sizeable German-Turkish population, Berlin remains a pretty white city compared to, say, London, where I lived before moving to Germany. So whenever I see a black person or someone from the Indian subcontinent, I often look up, delighted to feel a connection to back-home. I unintentionally make eye contact and then, to show that I'm happy to see them and am not being racist, I grin.

Of course all I'm doing is showing these people that I have recognised their otherness. I'm certain that none of these Berliners are delighted by the weird grinning Englishman who appears to think that they need his cheerful reassurance to feel welcome in their home city, in which he is the immigrant.

I do the same when I see what I assume to be two mothers with their child or two men walking down the street holding hands. Without Tom by my side, these strangers don't know that I'm a gay father; they just see a bearded dad pushing a pram and winking at them.

This rictus-grinned liberal-hearted positivity is a phenomenon that my husband and I call 'going all Frau Nowak' in honour of the eponymous branch manager of the local Commerzbank in Berlin who set up our first joint bank account in 2008 with such studied delight that we thought her teeth were going to fuse together.

The problem with these well-meaning responses, or rather the reason they make you feel uncomfortable, is that, in that brief interaction, you are being treated as an icon and not a person. You embody meaning, and that meaning hangs like a veil between you and your interlocutor.

When I sit opposite someone from Pakistan on the S-Bahn, hear them speak English on their telephone, I feel excited because they represent something to me about home and about values of multiculturalism and anti-racism that matter to me. These are values that this person would no doubt sympathise with. But in imbuing them with those values, I am making a fetish of them and I am not seeing them. This is well-meaning, warm-hearted racism. But it is racism none the less.

So when they get off the phone and I eventually manage to strike up a conversation, the conversation fails, because I am interested in what they represent, not who they are.

'Are you from the UK?' I say.

'No, Pakistan.'

'Oh. From Lahore? Islamabad?' I hear myself pronouncing it 'Islamabard', presumably in an attempt to sound knowledge-able and authentic.

'Lahore.'

'Big city.'

'Yes.'

Silence.

'Hot.'

'It can get hot.'

Silence.

So there are questions like the questions from the woman on the train that are hard to respond to, because she is not really asking me a question. She's asking 'Generic Gay Parent One' a question. Then there are the questions that reveal less about people's feelings towards same-sex parents – good or bad – and more about their expectations about fatherhood. The most common misjudged comment we get is some version of, 'Mum at home, is she?'

Usually I pretend to mishear, smile tightly or offer up that half laugh that one hopes will suffice as a universal response to comments one hasn't heard or wishes one hadn't. In the first few weeks of parenthood, though, after one 'Giving Mum a break, eh?' at the bakery and then a 'Mum putting up her feet, is she?' at the supermarket, I cracked.

I had met my friend Daniel for a coffee and was struggling

out of my extensive array of outerwear. One of my sense memories of London is the feeling of commuting on a rainy day; the specific sensation of cold dampness assailing you from the outside, meeting the hot dampness of your commuter sweat emanating from within. In Berlin, where it rarely rains but does get very cold, the equivalent feeling results from down-filled outerwear and very well-insulated buildings. It is the odd sensation, having come in from the cold, of sweating beneath your jumper as you desperately try to shed layer after layer of clothing, your ears and feet still numb.

Adding a baby into the mix, especially one strapped to your chest, makes this manoeuvre even more excruciating. And as I tried to drop my winter-duvet-weight down-jacket backwards onto a chair while pulling off Theo's hat and retrieving a lost glove with the toe of my boot, a man on the next-door table said, 'Mum's day off, is it?'

'He doesn't have a mum,' I snapped, silencing the chatter in the café.

The grandfather who'd asked paled and smiled. I sat down and, red-faced, unstrapped Theo from his baby carrier, awash with shame at my failure. For a start, it wasn't true: everyone was created by a father and mother, regardless of how they came into the world or in what kind of family constellation they ended up. Also, I was responding negatively about something Theo doesn't have, rather than offering up a simple: 'He has two dads.' But I couldn't explain all this to the grandad at the next-door table who was now studiously pushing the crumbs of his pain-au-chocolat around his plate with a cake fork.

The broader issue with these kinds of comment is not that everyone I bump into should be able to identify me as a gay father, but that their prevalence, however kindly meant, makes it clear that many people believe that fathers looking after children are just helping out the person who should actually be looking after the children. The mother.

The phrase that comes up most often – 'Mum's day off, is it?' – could not make it more explicit that childcare is conceived of as the mother's task, even when she's not doing it. When I relayed this story to my brother, he told me that whenever he tells someone he's staying in when my sister-in-law is out for the evening, they inevitably say, 'Oh, are you babysitting tonight?' 'No,' he has to reply, 'it isn't babysitting if it's your own child.'

What is stranger still is that these assumptions appear to be so firmly anchored in how people think about parenthood that, even when clearly faced with two dads, many people struggle to adjust their thinking.

In Germany, you have to hire a solicitor to submit your adoption documents and, when we visited ours to read through the details of the adoption application with our social worker, he said, with genuine friendliness, 'Well, I suppose, in the end, he'll be better off with you two than with his mother.'

As is often the case in these situations, I thought I was being oversensitive or had perhaps misheard or misunderstood. But our social worker chimed in: 'I should bloody well hope so.'

Was this in question for him? Was he cheerfully processing the adoption for a child he believed was being handed over to some pleasant-enough gay men, but that, really, the child should be being brought up by his mother who was sitting in some flat in Berlin wondering what she was going to do now that her baby had been taken away? He didn't know the details of Theo's case, but what did he imagine the social workers were up to? Removing children from their parents on a whim?

As we were getting Theo into his blue felt winter suit to leave, everyone managed to gather round me so that I got flustered and buttoned him up askew.

'You've missed a buttonhole,' Theo's social worker said.

The solicitor smiled and said, 'I suppose you do need a woman's eye for some things.'

Written here in black and white, these things sound pretty bad, especially from someone whom we'd just paid €100 for stamping a form. But he was such a friendly man, was genuinely nice to us, and genuinely seemed to be trying to do his best, that again I didn't respond. I only realised how off it was on the street when Theo's social worker said, 'Well, that was embarrassing for him.'

It was a lovely thing for her to say. Except that she was wrong. It was I who had been filled with embarrassment when I'd buttoned Theo's winter suit wrong. I don't think the solicitor had felt embarrassed about what he'd said at all. I think he thought he'd got the tone just right.

Even when I do manage a response to these kinds of comment, people are usually so oblivious to what they've said that I'm unable to engender any shame in them; it just goes over their head. When we were looking at flats when Theo was about six months old the estate agent showed us into a special downstairs room in the apartment block that had been set up for the residents to park their prams in. 'This is the room for the mums,' she said.

We were standing in front of her with a literal baby in a literal pram.

'Can dads use it too?' I asked.

She smiled at me benignly, completely missing the passive aggressive joke, and said, 'Oh sure. Anyone can use it.'

There is another type of question though.

The contrast to the mother on the train was the coat attendant at a large contemporary art gallery in Berlin. When the city's cultural institutions finally reopened after the first Covid lockdown, we took Theo in his pram for our first taste of city life in months. While I used the loo, Tom and Theo went to hand in our coats and the coat attendant, a peroxide-blonde Russian woman in her fifties, pointed at Theo and said to dark-haired Tom, 'All this beautiful blond hair must be from your wife.'

'He has two dads,' Tom responded.

'Two dads?' she repeated as I appeared around the corner. She had clearly never heard the like before. 'Do you think he will grow up to have girlfriends or boyfriends?' she asked, her brow ruffled in confusion.

'Who knows,' said Tom. 'Either would be fine.'

Why were my husband and I charmed by this deeply misguided question, but offended by a woman asking us a simple question about whether our son was adopted or not – a fact about his life that we are completely open about?

The reason was that the coat attendant had asked us a truly open question. She was not trying to show us that she either approved or disapproved of gay parents. She genuinely wanted to know if we thought that being raised by two dads was going to make him gay. And when we made it clear that we didn't think it would make any difference, she was happy to take our answer at face value and went on to get quite strict with us about buying woollen inserts for Theo's wellies.

'Cold comes up through the feet,' she told us. 'It can kill a child.'

So we have the good question, the open question, of genuine curiosity. Then we have the closed question, the question that is an act of social performance. And yet, even that mother on the train feeding her baby pretzels, asking us about how our child was conceived, showing us that she was 'OK' with us being gay parents – she was still greeting us and our situation positively. As was the mother from Theo's nursery who said,

'It's great that you guys are here – our daughter doesn't even know it's not normal.' As was the woman at the market who pointed to Tom and me with Theo in his sling and cheerfully said, 'We've got some of your lot in our building too.' As are the countless people who single us out to grin at on the playground, in cafés, on trains and in planes, trying to make us feel included but making us feel the opposite.

Is their goodwill meaningless because it is self-conscious? I suppose another way of addressing the same question would be to ask: although these interactions make me uncomfortable, to what extent can and should these people recognise that? They are certainly not trying to make me feel uncomfortable – quite the contrary, in fact.

Last year I went to a book reading where the author, also gay, was talking about how they deal with misplaced comments about their sexuality and gender. 'That's for straight people to sort out,' they said, 'it's their problem. We're just living our lives. Why is it always up to the person being marginalised to point out their persecution and to come up with the solution for it?'

I thought about this statement for a long time afterwards. It troubled me. Because I agreed with it wholeheartedly, in ethical and philosophical terms. And I feel it as someone from a marginalised group. I've spent years dealing with straight people's bigotry, wasted all that time and energy fighting off bullies at school and then endured countless demeaning comments and threatening situations as an adult. And now I have to fix it for them too? Now I have to tell the bigots what they need to do to feel better about themselves?

But then I'm also reminded of an episode of Esther Perel's wonderful couples therapy podcast *Where Should We Begin?*, in which she interrupts an arguing couple to ask whether they want to be right or they want to be married.

The 'it's not up to us to come up with a solution' line that that writer came up with could be reworded as the relationship classic: 'Well, if you don't know what the problem is, then there's no point in me telling you.' It's true. But it doesn't get us very far.

I also know that it doesn't square with my own experiences of prejudice. Without feminists, without anti-racists, without lesbian and trans activists, Jewish and Muslim commentators pointing out the ways in which they are marginalised and explaining to me how I could act differently, I would be a much more bigoted person, while remaining convinced that I was charming and enlightened. That I had all the answers.

And of course, in each of these interactions with what my husband and I perceive as 'normal' parents and 'normal' mothers, we are also making a set of assumptions that we could be equally criticised for. The mother on the train with the pretzels didn't tell us she was her child's biological mother. There are a few thousand 'rainbow families' in Germany but there are hundreds of thousands of children brought up by relatives: aunts and uncles, grandparents, siblings, elder brothers and sisters. Are these 'kinship' parents made to feel uncomfortable when I mistake them for the biological parents of the children they look after? I'm sure they are. Is it my fault for not recognising the potential diversity in their child–parent set-up? Perhaps. Perhaps it's time for me to do better too.

This, though, is surely an argument for us all to celebrate non-traditional families, to make them more visible in our TV shows, in our books and our films and our songs. I feel huge relief when I bump into one of the single parents in my son's nursery. I feel my shoulders relaxing, knowing that, for a moment, I don't have to think about whether I'm making anyone feel uncomfortable or challenged. It is the same when I bump into the step-mum, the same when I bump into the widower. And I hope too that their families, like our family, are a salve to the 'traditional' families. I hope that all non-traditional families, like our family, help 'traditional' families see how many of the pressures on their lives are based on social expectations that need not be fulfilled in order to build a loving home with well-adjusted, happy children.

## Out with the Baby

The concept of 'coming out' as gay has become such a cultural mainstay that it is now applied to any situation in which someone reveals something about themselves that might be perceived negatively by society at large. You can come out as an alcoholic,[4] come out as a conservative;[5] you can even 'come out of the broom closet' as a witch.[6] And for queer people, 'coming out' is increasingly understood as a challenging but essential and validating rite of passage through which they must pass, like some sort of gay bar mitzvah.

But the concept of 'coming out' is fraught. For a start, it is based on a binary notion of gay and straight and a single direction of travel. You reveal your sexual identity once, you cross the line from false-straight to true-gay and there you stay.

Quite apart from the fact that the notion of coming out ignores the fluidity inherent in all of our sexualities and how sexuality can subtly shift over time, it is also premised on the idea that it happens in a single moment, like a stamp in your passport. Clonk. Queer. But of course revealing your sexuality isn't something that happens in a single moment. Instead, queer people, like all invisible minorities, take part in a life-long negotiation with concealment and disclosure. Whenever I start a new job, find myself sitting next to someone I don't know at a wedding, go to a new doctor or dentist, I have to make a decision about when and if I will – for the hundredth time? the thousandth? – come out.

Why would you need to tell your dentist you're gay? you might ask. Well, the issue is that small talk often backs you into a corner.

'How are things, Herr Fergusson?'

'Oh, fine. A little tired.' (Appropriately vague.)

'A lot of work on?'

'No, it's the semester break, actually.' (Introduction of work topic to steer conversation back into safer waters.)

'You have a child?' (Uh-oh.)

'Yes.' (Concise. Not inviting questions.)

'Is your wife still breastfeeding?' (Cornered.)

Even the idea that 'coming out' reveals a truth is pretty dubious. Eve Sedgwick, one of the most celebrated proponents of what came to be known as queer theory, gave the example of two friends, a gay man and a straight woman, who, for a decade, talked to each other openly about their respective sex lives. But she had never referred to him as a 'gay man'. Ten years into their friendship, he came out to her. His coming out was not a moment of revelation – she already knew the details of his sex life. All he was doing was giving her permission to identify him as gay.[7]

Although Sedgwick was writing in the nineties, this is not some remnant of eras past when queer people felt less able to be open about their identities. I can think of a male friend in my wider circle of friends whom we have witnessed making out with members of the same sex and who has never had a girlfriend. I can think of another school friend who lives with a woman, owns a dog with her and, from her social media, is clearly out in her partner's circle of friends, but not in ours. We know they are queer. They know we know. But we don't acknowledge their queerness when we talk to them. If and when they do decide to come out to us it will not be revelatory; it will be a social signal. They will simply be giving us permission to talk about them in a certain way.

One thing that has changed since Eve Sedgwick wrote about her queer-but-not-out friend is that, by being given access to marriage and adoption, same-sex relationships have become bureaucratically recognised in many parts of the Western world and can, in fact, be rubber-stamped. As such, if you're queer, marriage and parenthood fundamentally change the way your visibility functions.

In some ways, things become easier. When you're single, it is quite difficult to drop into the conversation that you're gay without literally saying, 'Oh, I'm gay.' But when, as a woman, you mention your wife* the matter is dealt with.

There is a paradox in how my husband and I are seen in the world since we became parents. On the one hand, we are – as I described above – regularly mistaken for straight dads giving their wives a break. But this illusion is broken when we are parenting together in public – a job that often requires more than one set of hands. When my husband is pushing the pram and I am trying to get the dummy back into the baby's mouth the cover is blown. If our son is tired and refusing to ride his bright yellow pushbike and I'm carrying it while my husband is carrying him, it becomes obvious that we are a family.

The upshot is that, when I'm on my own with my son, I'm probably mistaken for straight more often than I was before

---

* The same is not true of German, in which the word for friend (*Freund*) is also the word for boyfriend. This is in itself massively telling of the expectations around gender and friendship, because this only functions because the term is gendered. So if a man talks about his *Freundin* (female friend) it is assumed he's talking about his girlfriend, because his 'friends' are obviously going to be other men. It is also really difficult to deal with as a non-native speaker, because people think you've made a mistake and assume you're just talking about a pal. 'You went to your friend's parents for Christmas again?' a woman in my German class asked me. 'But you were there at Easter. Don't you have your own family?'

I became a parent. But when I am parenting in public with my husband we are far more visible as a couple than we ever were without a child. This has, in turn, led us both to realise how invisible we had previously been. Indeed, I have been shocked by how fatherhood has exposed the extent to which Tom and I had hidden that we were a couple when we were in public.*

This was rarely something conscious. I never walk out of the house and think, 'I hope no one guesses I'm married to Tom.' But, as a gay person, you are trained through experience, like Pavlov's dogs, to keep your hands off your man.

This is in part because of what we don't see. If you think about it, at least every fifteenth couple you pass walking down the street holding hands should be a same-sex couple. This, of course, is not the case. In fact, if you have ever seen two men or two women walking down the street hand in hand, I suspect that it was such a novelty that you might even recall the exact occasion.

If the enforced invisibility of queer people is something that they themselves often underestimate, it's something that even the most enlightened straight people appear to be completely oblivious to.

In 2015, the (straight) English comedian Iain Lee had a call on his BBC Three Counties radio show[8] from a gay man who said he found it sad that he couldn't hold his boyfriend's hand in public. What was interesting about Lee's reaction was not that he was appalled, but that he 'didn't quite believe it'. Wasn't this the UK? Wasn't this the twenty-first century? So he took his male producer by the hand and set

---

* The dynamic, it is worth mentioning, functions differently for women. It is so normal to see a woman pushing a pram accompanied by another female friend or relative that lesbian parents I know are almost never recognised as a couple when they are together.

off into Luton, the Bedfordshire town in which the radio station is based.

Within minutes Lee noticed that people were staring at him and his producer. A dad with his daughter pulled his child away from them. And then a young man walked past them and said, 'Uurrgh.' This had all taken place within ten minutes. When Lee asked the man why he'd reacted that way, he said 'gays were wrong and that it was disgusting'.

Lee was chastened. But his disbelief was matched by my disbelief, when I read the article, that he was so unaware that that's what the reaction would be.

Of course, I'm aware because it happens all the time. My husband and I would only ever hold hands in public if we were somewhere we felt very safe, and even then we sometimes misjudge it. Someone shouted 'Fucking poofs!' at us when Tom took my hand in Soho a few years ago; a group of drunken men threatened to kill us on the Tube in central London when Tom put his hand on my knee; just two years ago, when we were walking with our baby through Viktoriapark in Kreuzberg, Berlin's most famously alternative district, a group of young men threatened to beat us up. Our crime: sharing an umbrella.

## The Myth of the New Man

In fairness to the grandad in the café and my brother's friends, the solicitor and the estate agent, the fathers of the world are rarely helping their cause when it comes to involving themselves in the benefits of shared parenthood. Because what was also striking to us when we first ventured onto the streets of Berlin with our son was that, other than Sundays on the playground – which appeared genuinely to be 'Mum's day off' – we almost never saw any other dads when our son was a small baby. I was ready to mostly see mothers, but was shocked, when I went to the doctor's, when I went to a baby music group, almost always to be the only father there.

This is especially striking in Germany where the financial barriers to fathers sharing childcare with their wives and partners are extremely low. A new parent receives twelve months of parental leave paid by the government at 70 per cent of their salary. To encourage fathers to take time off to help with childcare, the government also introduced a top-up of an extra two months added to this first year if both parents take parental leave, adding up to fourteen months in total. And these months can be overlapped, taken in blocks, separated as one desires.

We took seven months off each, overlapping two to cover the first months together. Your employer cannot refuse you taking these days. And if you so wish, this first twelve to fourteen months can represent the end of your full-time childcare duties. From one year old, your child is entitled to full-time childcare in a nursery, which is either free or heavily subsidised. In Berlin, a nursery can take your child from 7.30 a.m. to 6 p.m., five days a week, if you want, and you pay €23 a month for lunch and an afternoon snack.* On top of this, all parents in Germany receive €200 as a monthly cash payment, whatever their financial status, in addition to generous tax breaks for married couples and parents.

Despite these efforts, 70 per cent of fathers in Germany don't take a single day of paid parental leave.

Thank God, one might think, to be one of the lucky 30 per cent of mothers whose husbands deign to stop working

---

* In those federal states in which you have to pay for nursery, parents' annual childcare contributions are capped at around 6 per cent of their income. So in, say, Hessen, a family earning €50,000 would pay no more than €250 a month for nursery. To end up paying £1,100, the average monthly cost for nursery in the UK, you would have to be earning well over £200,000 a year.

for two months. Finally, Mum can go back to work before nursery kicks in, knowing that baby is safe at home with Dad. But I have only experienced this happening once. The trend in Germany is that the father overlaps his two months with the mother's last two months and they 'go travelling'. So instead of getting up with the baby and feeding her in the flat, Mum can spend two months getting up with the baby and feeding her on the step of a campervan with a view of Lake Constance.*

It is hard to express, when there is no social expectation about which parent should stay at home and look after the baby, how crazy the idea that either of you would do it single-handedly seems. If my husband had suggested going back to work full time after two weeks, I'd have thrown the television out the window.

The fact that women tend to take on the bulk of childcare is, of course, not news. But having to negotiate how my husband and I share childcare, without external pressure about who should do what, has made us acutely aware of the chasm between how people talk about shared parenting and how it pans out in the real world.

Mothers we know often tell us that they are splitting things fifty-fifty with their husband or partner. When they describe their weeks, though, it turns out that they meant fifty-fifty in the evenings and at weekends; and usually mothers did all the feeding. As the mother was the constant, she inevitably became the only person who could comfort the child, so she was still doing most parenting even when the father was around.

Bringing up children isn't a science, and however hard my husband and I try, we can't split the childcare exactly

---

* The iconic image of this approach to parental leave was the Austrian politician who tweeted a picture of himself alone on the ski slopes with the caption 'Last day of parental leave'.

fifty-fifty. He is at his therapy practice three days a week; I work part time at a university for two. Until Theo went to nursery at the age of two, I was writing during his nap times and in the evenings.

There are some things that one of us finds easier than the other. I've always enjoyed cooking and end up feeding our son more often. Now that the three of us eat the same meal in the evening, I'm doing nearly all the cooking. My husband does more bedtimes. I clean the bathroom. He takes out the bins. He used to do the laundry, but now there's far too much of it and we both end up feeding the washing machine daily, like a pair of steam-engine stokers. But we both do everything at least once or twice a week, and spend a big chunk of time alone with our son.

At its simplest, sharing childcare has a massive practical benefit. No one is ever taking on everything and there is always relief around the corner. When Theo wakes up at five in the morning – and I have pulled myself upright to spend three seconds sitting on the edge of the mattress gathering enough energy and mental wherewithal to cheerfully respond to my son's surprised 'Still dark, Dada' when I open his curtains – I know that tomorrow, the next day maybe, Tom will be on duty and I will be able to pull the covers over my head and bliss out until 8.30 a.m.*

But there is also a huge, enveloping feeling of security that comes from bringing up a child with a parent who you know has all the skills to fully cover you should you be out of action.

I constantly hear stories, amusingly told, by friends who are

---

* Originally, the simple rule was that one person got up with him and one person got a lie-in. The problem was that we were both so tired that the person lying in would simply sleep through until 11 a.m., just in time for Theo to go down for his first nap. Eventually we negotiated a weekend lie-in of 8.30 a.m. as late enough to feel like you'd got a bit of extra rest, but early enough that you could still contribute to morning parenting.

mothers about leaving their child with their husband for the day and returning at three in the afternoon to discover everyone still in their pyjamas and the baby's nappy unchanged. I used to laugh along heartily to stories of inept dads sitting their children on the kitchen counter top to feed them and going to answer the door while the child plopped face-first to the floor – ho ho ho – or inventing a game that involved dragging their giggling baby around on the carpet only to discover they had worked up a huge bleeding carpet burn on the back of the baby's head – hee hee hee.

Now I just feel anxious at the thought of these mothers raising a child with someone who isn't just as concerned about their welfare as they are; feeling that there is no one else in the world who could or would care as well for this child as they would.

I think that's how most mothers feel, and it must be terrifying.


## An Extended Simile

This all makes me think of posh people and money.

I went to school in Didcot, a very average railway town in Oxfordshire with a power station, a one-sided high street and a very mixed social demographic.* It meant that, long before I was old enough to notice the import of these things, I would go to sleepovers at a friend's pebble-dashed council house, where we slept on mattresses on the floor with their four siblings, in the same week as I'd been splashing around in another friend's indoor pool and taking turns being led round a paddock on their little sister's pony.

---

\* Didcot is in fact so average that it is the locality in the UK that most perfectly reflects the voting intentions of the rest of the country.

I was the son of a doctor and a village kid, so firmly counted as one of the poshos. My friend Gareth lived in the sprawling new estate north of the town, where he was raised by his single mum. He was not counted as one of the poshos. This didn't mean very much to either of us when we met at the age of eleven, other than that people often took the piss out of me for pronouncing 'really' as 'rarely'.

When we left school, though, it suddenly meant a lot. Gareth and I both got pretty good A Level results and won places at nice Russell Group universities – me doing English at Warwick, him doing Geography at Birmingham just half an hour down the road. But Gareth never made it to Birmingham. Instead, he deferred and got a job for what was supposed to be just twelve months to make enough money to help pay for his first year of study. But at the end of that first year, the company offered to keep him on and he dropped his university place. I was heartbroken and confused as our destinies suddenly diverged.

In 1998, tuition fees were still low and were means-tested, so he wouldn't have had to pay them. He had already arranged his student loan and wouldn't have started paying it back until he was earning a reasonable wage after graduation. These, of course, were the classic arguments of the politicians who decided to cancel student grants and introduce university tuition fees a few years earlier.

Armed with this knowledge, I tried to talk Gareth into going. It seemed to me like a no-brainer. His response: he was terrified of stretching himself so thin without any kind of back-up. If he was suddenly a few hundred quid short he wouldn't be able to feed himself and pay his rent. He might be evicted and lose his university place anyway. If I was two hundred quid down, I could just phone home.

'But I'd never do that,' I said.

'But you could.'

At eighteen, I realised for the first time that the real power of money in my life was not that we had two spare rooms, but that I had been gifted a mental security blanket. That I knew, deep down, that, however badly things went, however financially stretched I was, I could – to paraphrase Jarvis Cocker – call my dad and he could stop it all.

This, I think, is how parenthood must feel for most mothers. A sense that, if it all goes pear-shaped, there's no one to call. There's no one who is ever going to look after your child – who's going to love them, even – as well and as instinctively as you can.

I'm not saying for a second that most dads don't love their kids; indeed, I think most dads love their kids more than any other person in their lives. And maybe most mums think that, in the end, if something happened to them, Dad would roll up his sleeves and do a great job parenting on his own. But they couldn't be sure. Because they'd never seen him do it.

Don't get me wrong – splitting parenthood down the middle leads to a lot of tit-for-tat arguments. There is plenty of 'Oh, do you let him do his own teeth?' and 'I was just wondering why you wanted him to eat so much salt'. But, throughout the highs and lows of parenthood, I've had someone not just by my side, but shoulder to shoulder with me. Someone as star-struck and in love with our son as I am, but also just as concerned, just as worried, just as ready to jump in and help when things go wrong.

# Consolations

## The Consolations of Parenthood

On my father's side, we are the atheists in a family of believers. When my gran died, she wanted to be buried next to my grandad, but no one in the family could remember where in the churchyard we'd buried Grandad four decades earlier. 'Well, who's the church warden?' someone asked. It was my aunt, but she'd only taken over a week earlier. 'And who was the church warden before you?' someone said. 'Gran,' was the reply. 'And before her?' someone asked. 'Grandad.' The reason, in fact, that we couldn't find him was that he hated mowing around the gravestones when he was the church warden so refused to have one of his own.

So most of my father's family is strongly Church of England. Both of my uncles abandoned Anglicanism to become born-again Christians; they preach in evangelical churches in Australia and New Zealand. But my father became a surgeon, married into a family of surgeons, and we were raised agnostically.

My siblings and I were educated in Church of England state schools where Moses and Jesus were one part of a pantheon of semi-mythical figures, from King Arthur to Robin Hood, that we all assumed were meant to be addressed with the same degree of friendly scepticism.

In our village in South Oxfordshire, religion was never aggressively rejected, but belief in God fell away as one grew up, as it did for the Tooth Fairy or Father Christmas. At secondary school in Didcot, people who held on to religion in any serious kind of way were seen as rather infantile. They were people who couldn't accept the very obvious reality that you just die and that's it. They were people who had to believe in heaven, in life-after-death, because they were too dumb or too frightened to face the harsh reality of their mortality.

'I suppose I don't really believe that it all just ends when you do' was about the most ardent statement of faith you might hear from your friends as you philosophised on your back in a field, staring at the stars while you swigged from a two-litre bottle of White Lightning.

For me, though, the promise of heaven has never particularly been the attraction of religion. The thought of eternity is what terrifies me. Eternal life or eternal death – I don't find either concept particularly comforting. But as a naturally anxious person, what I find hugely comforting in the idea of a faith is God's plan. The idea that I am not solely responsible for my few successes and prodigious failures. The idea that, at the end of the day, I did not have to worry that I had done enough; that there was a plan for me, which I didn't need to try and comprehend, because I couldn't comprehend it – it passeth all understanding. 'Trust in the Lord with all thine heart; and lean not unto thine own understanding. In all thy ways acknowledge him, and he shall direct thy paths.'[1] What a blessed relief.

For me, the great consolation of parenthood is that it answers these very same anxieties. I am not for a second suggesting that parenthood is not anxiety-provoking. From the day we brought Theo home, I have felt as if someone has removed my wet, beating heart and set it toddling off to the nearest sharp corner. But parenthood is extremely structuring and there is a great security to be found in that.

The first time I had a hint of the joys of this overwhelming responsibility was when Tom and I were living in the UK and we looked after my niece and nephew for a weekend while my sister and brother-in-law went to a wedding. It was a full-on, glass-of-water-in-the-face introduction to childcare. Going to bed with the expectation that I wasn't going to be sleeping through the night. Waking up and having to be instantly mobile and verbal. Hearing my stomach squelch and looking at the clock to see whether it was lunchtime yet and realising that it wasn't even 9 a.m.

But there was a moment in the late afternoon, when my niece was watching a cartoon, my nephew watering plants in the garden with my husband, and I was cooking dinner. It was a moment in the day around six o'clock when I would usually begin the process of reflecting on all the things I had failed to achieve that day and weighing up what I could possibly get done before I went to bed. Today, though, there were two little children who had to be fed. I had to feed them, then bring them to bed. I had no choice about what I was going to focus on for the next three hours. Emotionally, morally, logically and legally my priorities were completely fixed. And it filled me with a wave of deep relaxation.

Since our son arrived, I have never felt older or more exhausted. Caring for him is relentless. I have never been a man who loves a swift transition. Before I had a kid, I used to set my alarm to go off an hour before I actually had to start getting ready for work, so that I could slope to the kitchen, make tea and crawl back into bed to read until I felt able to face showering.

Now, every morning I shift from deep, black sleep to 'AWAKE!' shouted in gravelly German over the baby phone. Be it 5.30 or 8.30, I have to be instantly conscious, changing a nappy, reading him a book, making breakfast, my vision still blurry with sleep.

I sit down to pee with my head in my hands just to have a break, but my son pads in with a book.

We play hide and seek and I hide myself under the covers well enough not to be found for a minute so that I can just lie there in the uterine darkness as he wanders the flat calling my name.

I go to our bedroom to plug my phone in to charge and let myself lean against the pillow for long enough to allow me to scroll through a few banal Instagram feeds until my husband shouts, 'Ben?'

I pretend not to hear.

'Be-en? Where are you?'

I get my shoulders onto the pillow. I hear, 'Go and find Dada,' and my son's little heels drum across the floor as he homes in on me like a cruise missile.

It is exhausting. It is overwhelming. But I am not wondering where I need to be or what I need to do. My task is clear. There was once a decision. It was about whether or not to become a parent, and it happened a long time ago. But that feels like something prehistoric, something for the archaeologists to pick over.

I am immersed in parenthood. I am in it over my head. There will be a day, no doubt, when he heads off on a first school trip or goes to university and I will emerge dripping on the other side, wondering what has happened to me these past decades. But for now, I have a plan that passeth all understanding. And that makes me very content indeed.

## The Consolations of Motherhood

Countering men who think that their wife or girlfriend should be the primary caregiver when their wife or girlfriend wants to share childcare is relatively unproblematic. The men are obviously wrong.

Some would argue that, as long as women carry and give birth to children, as long as breastfeeding remains the healthiest way of feeding a baby, mothers will always be taking on more childcare than fathers. It is a fact rooted in biology.

This argument begins to look a little shaky, however, when we consider how many women actually breastfeed. In most Western countries, 20 per cent of children are never breastfed. In the USA over 25 per cent of children never receive breastmilk and in some European countries, such as Ireland, 45 per cent of babies are never breastfed.[2] And in many countries, including the UK, in which a majority of women begin breastfeeding, most do not breastfeed past the six-week mark.[3] In these countries, there is thus no part of the childcare routine that a father could not be assuming after the first month or so.

Nevertheless – one might counter – after the initial bonding of pregnancy and breastfeeding, not to mention the 45 per cent or so of mothers who do continue to breastfeed in the longer term, childcare is always going to be weighted towards mothers. The scales of childcare will always tip towards Mum.

This may be the case, but we're not just talking about an imbalance. The stay-at-home father is a unicorn; he remains the stuff of legend. In 2019, less than 5 per cent of fathers in the UK had reduced their working hours to cover *any* amount of childcare, let alone dropped work completely to look after their kids.[4] In the US, families in which the father was the sole breadwinner shrunk dramatically from 47 per cent in 1970 to just 27 per cent in 2016. But this was not accompanied by a concomitant shift in fathers staying at home to look after their kids. In the States, stay-at-home dads increased from 4 per cent in 1989 to 7 per cent of fathers in 2016.

'Just a moment,' you cry, 'seven per cent of fifty million American families is a lot of stay-at-home dads.' True, but only 24 per cent of those stay-at-home dads gave childcare as the main reason that they were staying at home, giving us a figure of just 1.68 per cent of American families headed by stay-at-home dads who were there primarily to look after their kids and not, say, because they happened to be retraining or unemployed.[5]

'But wait!' you screech. 'What about Scandinavia?' And, yes, Nordic countries are streets ahead of the rest of the world in terms of sharing parental leave. All Scandinavian countries offer over forty weeks of paid leave that can be split between both parents, with Sweden offering the most at sixty-nine weeks. I remember visiting Sweden about ten years ago and being struck by the number of dads I saw around Stockholm pushing prams and feeding babies – something I had rarely seen in London at the time. But even our friends in the North have not yet managed to completely shed the traditional split of working father and stay-at-home mother. Finnish and Danish fathers only take around 11 per cent of the paid paternity leave they are entitled to take, Norwegian fathers around 20 per cent and Swedish and Icelandic fathers around 30 per cent. Indeed, almost 80 per cent of mothers in these countries are taking more than six months of childcare leave compared to only 5 per cent of fathers.[6]

Anecdotally, from my urban, liberal bubbles in London and Berlin, I have heard tale after tale of fathers not enraged that they were being asked to share childcare, but rather stunned at the idea that they weren't already doing enough.

I think of a friend whose husband fled the stifling

conservatism of rural Germany for Berlin, but was baffled by and then indignant at her suggestion that, when she stopped breastfeeding, he could start sharing the night feeds. A friend whose husband was bewildered when she suggested that he might drop a couple of days of work to help look after the baby, since she earned more and it made sense for her to be the one working full time. The numerous female friends who, desperate not to come across as nags, simply gave up asking their partners to do the most basic of household tasks after the baby arrived, from picking up their clothes to taking the bins out.

I understand these men too, of course. It is that age-old question of privilege that every single one of us has to face at some point in our lives. We all experience our own reality of joy and pain and it is a horrible feeling when someone adds to our burden by turning up a problem in some previously unmarred part of our lives.

When my brother, my sister and I were sixteen, twelve and fourteen respectively my parents went to a dinner party and witnessed the hosts' teenage children filling the dishwasher. Inspired, they announced around the dinner table the following evening that none of us had ever had chores and it wasn't really fair that Mum cooked us dinner every night and then had to clean the kitchen too. So from now on we had to do our own laundry and, on one week night each, we had to fill the dishwasher after dinner.

We greeted this suggestion with stunned silence. And then rage.

'Why?'

'Who *are* these people?'

'No one's *asking* you to cook every night.'

'You *like* cooking.'

'You can't *make* us do anything.'

'*I'll* do the cooking and *you* can do the dishes.'

'This isn't fair.'

'This has come out of *nowhere*.'

'No one *asked* you to have children.'

'I'll just make myself sandwiches from now on.'

But fuelling our anger was the realisation, deep down, that we had been getting away with not lifting a finger for years. We had been made aware of our deeply held belief that it was Mum's job to clean up after us. It was a belief that we had never had to question. And bubbling up inside each of us was the thought: If we begin to pick at that thread, where will it end? We could be working in factories by the end of the week.

So the appalled father, knocked out of his privilege, we understand. Liberally minded fathers have, over the decades, come to accept as normal that their wives and girlfriends work. They have become accustomed to being able to change the odd nappy. Some even cook, help with the school runs, bring their children to bed. But I have never met a single straight couple with children in which childcare is shared equally and in which both parents have the same professional status and earnings in their relationship. For a *Guardian*-reading, urban-dwelling homosexual who has only ever worked in female-dominated industries, that is remarkable. It is not an imbalance; it's a scam.

The issue is that waves of feminism have opened up more and more opportunities for women and their lives have been transformed, but this has not been balanced out by a revolution in the social role of men. Women have broken into the board-room, achieved the highest political office in many countries, but if they have children they are still expected to be dedicated mothers. And if they do not have children, they are expected to explain why.

Women's lives have changed radically, but we have not asked men to radically change their lives in return. My grandmother looked after the home and the children while my grandfather went out to work full time. My mother took seven years off work to look after us, then went back to work, while my father went out to work full time. My sister took three years off work, then went back to work part time, while her husband went out to work full time.

There is no question that these three generations of fathers have gradually taken on more childcare. My grandfather had no involvement in his children's care. My father was completely able to bathe us and feed us if my mum was out, but never did if she was home. My sister's ex-husband shares custody with my sister and is as involved with the kids as she is when he's not working. But he still went back to work full time after a week or two at home with each baby. And none of these women were ever able to recover their earnings up to the level of their husbands'. My sister's life as a mother looks completely different from my gran's life as a mother. But my brother-in-law's life as a father is a tweaked version of my grandfather's. It is not a transformation.

What is much harder to address, as a man stepping into a traditionally female role, are all the small ways in which mothers benefit from being the primary caregiver to their children. The challenge when living a life that questions a patriarchal model of what a family should look like – particularly when the shape of your family questions the 'traditional' role of the mother – is that motherhood offers many consolations and those consolations are, in a number of ways, profoundly satisfying. That is to say, not only are many women invested in 'traditional' conceptions of motherhood, but actually stand to lose something if it was radically reshaped.

History is littered with the stories of more powerful people repressing, not the less powerful, but those whose power they have managed to limit. The most egregious of these relationships, like slavery, offer no consolations; those who defend slavery are always the perpetrators. No slave has ever been a great apologist for slavery. If we think about the centuries it took to ban slavery and the fact that it is still endemic throughout the world today in myriad covert forms, it is no surprise that exploitative power-relationships that are more ambiguous are even harder to crack.

Emotionally, the most powerful consolation to a mother of being the primary or sole caregiver is, I think, becoming, for a decade at least, the most important person in someone's life. I experience snatches of this. It is awful seeing your child upset, but there is also a deep pleasure to be found in your child facing a difficult situation and only being able to comfort itself by coming to you. There is a feeling of profound emotional power in knowing that your being, your embrace alone, is enough to completely heal another person's heartache.

This is true for me when I'm out with my son, on the playground or at nursery. But by sharing parenthood with my husband, we both miss out on being parent-in-chief. I am not the only person in the world who can comfort him. It is true that our son is happiest when we are both home. When he cries in the night, he wants to be brought back to our bed and fall asleep between us. But if one of us is away, he is interested in where the other one is ('Papa working?') but he doesn't pine. He is happy with the dad who's left over.

The same is not true of mums. I have had many conversations with tired, beaten-down mothers whose eyes sparkle a little when they relate how they left their children in their husband's care for an hour and came home to their child screaming for their mother.

'He just needs his mum,' they will say to me, smiling with guilty joy.

# Identity

The matriarch, the mother, has a great symbolic power in the family and in every society in the world. But the problem with being a symbol is that there is very little room for you. To fully achieve a completely essential role in the eyes of your children, not to mention society, you have to give up everything, including your sense of self.

I have found it striking since Theo has started nursery how often my experiences of parenthood mirror those of the mothers I chat to as we wrestle our children into their winter clothes. I knew that having two dads was not going to be completely different from having a mum and a dad, but in the fundamentals – in the things you do, the worries you have, the problems you face – far more connects us than divides us.

The first weeks with our son were very different, because we had not experienced any physical trauma. My friends who had Caesareans couldn't sit up in bed when they got home from hospital; one friend's scar didn't heal and she had to be filled with antibiotics and restitched again. Another was stuck in hospital for days on end dealing with her son's and her own infections and complications before she was allowed to take him home. A number made it back home soon after the first birth only for mastitis to turn their breasts to stone and give them forty-degree fevers. None of these women were snuggled up into bed to convalesce while their husbands slipped down the stairs with the baby in their arms. The message was clear: you're a mother now, so you'd better get bonding and feeding, even if you literally can't walk and it feels like you're being knifed in the tit.

My husband and I were mentally overwhelmed, but we didn't have stitches and haemorrhoids, healing wounds and cracked nipples. The experience of adoption is intensely emotional. And burgeoning research on fathers who are also primary caregivers has shown that fathers experience similar hormonal and cognitive changes to biological mothers when they become parents.[7] But our emotions, whether they were driven by hormones or the experiences we were going through, were not directly preceded by a physical experience of extreme metamorphosis and pain. An experience that, in any other circumstances, someone would be allowed years to process before they were given a task as physically and psychologically strenuous as looking after a baby. How often I have seen friends being asked about their births and seen them respond with wide eyes and silent tears.

So in those first weeks we were deeply privileged with our bodies that, if not well-oiled machines, certainly looked and felt much the same as the bodies we had inhabited before we became parents. After a few weeks, though, as the mothers around us healed, the lack of sleep began to envelop us too and we were able to slip into the zombie-like comradeship of the parents in our neighbourhood. Our tiredness was the same. Our adoration was the same. Our anxieties about our son's health were the same. But our sense of self has remained intact and this has not been the case for many of our female friends.

Just last week, as the first crocuses pushed through the black earth in the park by our flat, we bumped into an old work colleague pushing her eighteen-month-old in his pram.

'Oh, I got a nursery place,' she said.

'Oh brilliant! Which one did you get into?'

'The Rudolf Steiner nursery.'

It was a lovely nursery, although certainly the most new-age we had looked at. The children had to eat their breakfast outside in all weathers and if they couldn't fall asleep during nap time the nursery teachers massaged their feet with essential oils.

'And then,' our neighbour said, hand on hip, looking wistfully off into catkin-strewn bushes, 'I'll have to have a think about what *I* like doing.'

'In what sense?'

A breeze still with a wet touch of winter cold moved the soft black curls at her neck.

'Well,' she said, 'his dad took him for three hours at the weekend so that I could have a break. And I didn't have a clue what to do. I'm not even sure I can remember what I like doing. I feel like I've got to find myself again.'

I have heard some version of this a hundred times since becoming a parent. And I recognise in it something I've heard a thousand times more on countless reality shows since the 1990s. It is always the plucky mother of three kids in her forties or fifties who says, 'I was a mum for twenty years. And now I want to do something for myself. I want to find out what I'm capable of.'

I have never heard any father utter anything close. Being a dad matters socially, of course, but a father is not expected to subsume his former identity in his new role as a dad. Fathers are not expected to stop being ambitious, to sacrifice not only their bodies at the altars of their children but also their minds. They are not expected to shed their former personas like a lizard sheds its skin only to recall their former selves like something remembered from a dream.

In *A Life's Work*, Rachel Cusk describes the first months of her life with her newborn child thus:

I cohabit uneasily with myself, with the person I was before. I look at this person's clothes, her things. I go through her memories, like an imposter, prurient and faintly scandalised. Her self-involvement, her emotional vulnerability alarm me. I inhabit her loves, her concerns with the detachment of a descendant piecing together family history, with the difference that these concerns still live: I am importuned by them; they require my involvement.[8]

It is one of the few areas of the parental experience in which I see almost no crossover between straight mothers and myself. It's of course the case that there are hundreds of things that my husband and I used to do, used to enjoy doing, and no longer do. We barely eat out or go to museums, we haven't travelled in three years other than to visit our families. We talk wistfully of the feeling of popcorn beneath our shoes in the cinema, of the floating half wakefulness of a lie-in, of weekends spent trying to summon the energy to do something useful, but knowing that doing nothing was completely possible. But we haven't forgotten that we enjoyed doing those things.

If I have an afternoon to myself I go and eat a sake ikura don at a cheap Japanese restaurant, visit the English Bookshop in Berlin-Mitte and – time permitting and pandemics allowing – go to the cinema. It's exactly what I did before I had a kid.

I do not mean to say that fatherhood hasn't changed me. In fact, as someone who didn't have children for a long time, I am often rather ashamed by how changed I am. I used to scoff at my mother for being squeamish about TV crime dramas that involved children being hurt or kidnapped; charmed and disbelieving when my mother and grandmother wept in front of any act of kindness or cruelty in any film or television programme we watched. But, since we brought Theo home, I sense in myself that same flicked switch. Without being able to explain it in psychological terms, I feel emotionally invested in the world at some primal level I don't understand.

I see a poster of a wide-eyed, pot-bellied child in a refugee camp. The image, which I had always understood to be a symbol of disaster, is suddenly just someone's child who doesn't have enough to eat.

On the way to pick up my son from nursery, I listen to a BBC History podcast about an Iraqi mother who lost all her children when an American missile hit the Amiriyah bomb shelter in Baghdad during the First Gulf War and I begin to cry so hard that I have to stop walking and compose myself.

I read just the headline of a story on my news app about a baby that died after being left out in the cold on a balcony in Siberia and it haunts me for days.

But when the mothers I know say to me 'I don't really know who I am any more', I can empathise, but I can't uncover that feeling in myself.

Imagine a man you love, a father, saying those same words to you. 'I don't really know who I am any more.'

Wouldn't it be a crisis? Wouldn't you feel that parenthood had asked too much of him? Wouldn't you rush into action and try to save him?

## Equal Parenting

So what would genuinely equitable parenting look like for straight parents?

It might begin with a conversation before conception about how parenting was going to be approached. Together, our parents would dispense with all assumptions about who might do what and then create a vision of their future family dividing up tasks based on what they want and what they are good at. If at this point Mum wants to stop working during parental leave and Dad is happy with that, then of course that's fine. If Mum wants to start working again after two months, that's fine too.

When the baby arrived, our husband and wife might take off the first two months of parental leave together. In the first weeks when Mum was convalescing, and if she was breast-feeding, Dad would be doing almost everything else in the house and would be covering nappy changing and bathing alone, so that Mum could focus on feeding and recovering from birth. After the first two months of parental leave, Mum and Dad would divide the remaining leave in two in whatever order and constellation functioned best for both parents.

If they were lucky enough to live in a country where paid childcare was available to them, they would split that allow-ance. If not, they would both go back to work part time whenever that was practical.

Within the relationship, childcare would not be under-stood by either parent as being the same as work; it would be understood as being harder than work. The work of the parent at home begins with the first cry of their child and continues mercilessly until their child is tucked back into bed again. The parent going to work is faced with a day full of golden little pauses. Listening to the radio or reading a book on their commute, going to the toilet on their own, thinking about what they want to eat, pootling about online or on their phone for a few minutes between meetings, chatting with colleagues.

If there is an earning imbalance, this would not mean the lower-earning parent simply stops working. Their work mat-ters. It will be compensated for in the lower-earning parent covering the extra day of the five-day week in a way that is proportional to the earning imbalance. If Dad was earning more, he would look after baby for two days maybe, Mum three. If Mum was earning more, it would be the other way round. They would make less money than they would if the higher earner worked full time, but they will have made allowance for this when they were deciding together whether they could afford to have a baby.*

At this point, you may be feeling uncomfortable. You may be thinking, So if Mum's the higher earner she's going to be looking after her baby less just so the family can earn more?

It's an odd thought, isn't it? And yet we would not find it odd if these were high-powered, wealthy parents – celebrities, perhaps – who hired a nanny so that they could both go back to work after two months. Think about what that means: we are more comfortable with the idea of a stranger looking after someone's child than that child's own father looking after them.

As our couple's child grew up, they would continue to share parenting, bedtimes and household tasks. None of this would be done arbitrarily, but with a continual focus on what each parent did well and what each parent liked doing.

Vital to the ongoing success of our couple's balanced parenting would be a kind of maintenance of the parental unit which would involve Mum and Dad constantly shielding themselves emotionally and psychologically from the relentless social pressure to default back to a 'traditional' model of motherhood.

This sounds like a pretty reasonable division of labour. Not right for everyone, but a good baseline to work from. But I only know one couple who've been able to get anywhere close.

---

* Until I had a child, I had always bought the argument that women inevitably end up taking more time off work for parental leave than men because the man is nearly always the higher earner. If we just cracked pay inequality, I thought, then things would even themselves out. But when we actually had the discussion about who was going to take off how much time, with no gender expectations involved, I was struck by the fact that our relative earnings were part of the conversation, but by no means the whole conversation. I earn less than my husband, but I had no interest in completely giving up my job for two years just because I brought home a bit less than he did. Why should I be punished for having a job that pays a bit less? I was much more prepared for us to tighten our belts a little bit than for me to quit working completely.

In that family, Mum took the bulk of parental leave for the first child and Dad the bulk of parental leave for the second. And even then, Mum really struggled with the thought that she was doing the wrong thing by going back to work.

## The Traditional Family

When we are suggesting changes to the traditional family, it is important to remind ourselves that the 'traditional' family as it is figured today is not traditional at all. If we go back to the first half of the last century we will find middle-class families employing nannies to raise their children and cooks to make them their dinner. Mothers like Bertha in Katherine Mansfield's story 'Bliss', completely divorced from the raising of her own baby:

> 'She's been a sweet all the afternoon,' whispered Nanny. 'We went to the park and I sat down on a chair and took her out of the pram and a big dog came along and put its head on my knee and she clutched its ear, tugged it. Oh, you should have seen her.'
>
> Bertha wanted to ask if it wasn't rather dangerous to let her clutch at a strange dog's ear. But she did not dare to. She stood watching them, her hands by her side, like the poor little girl in front of the rich little girl with the doll.
>
> The baby looked up at her again, stared, and then smiled so charmingly that Bertha couldn't help crying:
>
> 'Oh Nanny, do let me finish giving her supper while you put the bath things away.'
>
> 'Well, M'm, she oughtn't to be changed hands while she's eating,' said Nanny. 'It unsettles her; it's likely to upset her.'[9]

And after seven challenging years of arm's-length childcare, Bertha would no doubt have tearfully waved her children off to boarding school; the scant responsibilities of parenthood would become the work of Christmas, Easter and summer holidays.

Even in developed nations, the vast majority of families in the early to mid-twentieth century were not, of course, middle-class. But working-class mothers were still not sat at home mothering their children alone while their husbands were out at work. As the politician Alan Johnson recalled, reflecting on his childhood in Notting Hill, then a deprived district of West London:

> We were used to being left alone from an early age because poor Lily never stopped working [. . .] A myth seems to have taken root in our retrospective view of the 1950s that women didn't work outside the home and that the husband was always the breadwinner. That may have been the convention in middle-class households, but it certainly wasn't the case in the working-class families in our street.[10]

The little support that working-class families received in 1950s London came largely from what Michael Young and Peter Willmott famously referred to as 'kinship groups' – extended family networks in working-class urban areas helping to raise each other's children.[11] Grandparents, great-uncles, aunts, cousins and multiple children often lived in the same houses and neighbourhoods. Older children helped raise younger children and the moment a child was able to fend for themselves, the back door was opened in the morning and they were told to stay out until tea time.

This pattern of communities supporting the children of mothers who work was and remains commonplace in non-white communities in Western countries. Black women in

North America and Europe continue to be deeply involved in raising children collectively in what Patricia Hill-Collins calls 'other mothering'. These kinship relationships were not and are not celebrated in the West; indeed, black parenting in the form of the black working mother and absent black father is still widely cited by politicians and commentators alike as a key driver of urban and social decline. As the academic Tracey Reynolds points out, 'As black mothers, we are more likely to work full-time to make up [the] economic shortfall, which emerges out of black women's subordinate structural location. Yet, persistent cultural messages tell us that the maternal ideal is still that of the stay-at-home/part-time worker mother whose primary role is domestic home care provider.'[12]

So our image of the 'traditional' family as working father and stay-at-home mother is also a white one. Or rather, it is a white one based in part on a very selective reading of non-white family forms. Because the marketing of baby-wearing cloths to whole parenting concepts is often based on a reading of parenting in, say, Africa as being more 'natural' and less industrialised than urban parenting in the West, ignoring the fact that most African mothers who carry their babies around with them in cloths do so because they have work to do;[13] the five countries with the highest rates of female participation in the workforce – Tanzania, Madagascar, Rwanda, Mozambique and Zimbabwe – are, in fact, all in Africa.[14]

So when we hear people defending 'traditional' motherhood, we have to remember that the modern-day 'traditional' mother – struggling alone, trying not to lose her mind while her husband's at work – is a Western invention of the last fifty years. This is not how our grandmothers were being raised; it was not how they were raising our parents. This is not how children are being raised in Kigali or Dar es Salaam. It may be true that there's nothing traditional about dads changing their children's nappies. But there's also nothing traditional about mums quitting work to take care of their children all by themselves while trying to stave off crippling loneliness.[15]

One of the most difficult things about critiquing how damaging many elements of modern-day motherhood are is that it entails questioning some of the thinking that underpins issues like 'natural' birth, breastfeeding and attachment parenting.

These concepts are not in themselves problematic. A mother who gives birth to her child at home without medical intervention, who breastfeeds until her child is two, who binds her child to her body, carrying them until they are able to walk – that mother will no doubt raise a healthy, secure and happy child. I understand too that the proponents of these theories during the fifties, sixties and seventies, like Mary Ainsworth and Jean Liedloff, were reacting to a world in which childcare had become infiltrated by modern, male-dominated medical systems that treated childbirth in the same terms as appendectomies.

When I think about men's slow medicalisation of childbirth over the last few centuries, I imagine it like a colonisation. All those male doctors in white coats travelling up the vagina and giving their name to every organ they passed – the Fallopian tubes, the pouch of Douglas, the glands of Montgomery – like Cecil Rhodes furnishing every street, institution and land in southern Africa with his moniker.

My image of the male medicalisation of childbirth is Sylvia Plath's description of Esther Greenwood visiting her medical-student boyfriend, Buddy, and witnessing for the first time a woman giving birth, seeing a 'dark fuzzy thing' appearing 'through the split, shaven place between her legs, lurid with disinfectant':

She seemed to have nothing but an enormous spider-fat stomach and two little ugly spindly legs propped in the high stirrups, and all the time the baby was being born she never stopped making this unhuman whooing noise.

Later Buddy told me that the woman was on a drug that would make her forget she'd had any pain and that when she swore and groaned she really didn't know what she was doing because she was in a kind of twilight sleep.

I thought it sounded just like the sort of drug a man would invent. Here was a woman in terrible pain, obviously feeling every bit of it or she wouldn't groan like that. And she would go straight home and start another baby, because the drug would make her forget how bad the pain had been, when all the time, in some secret part of her, that long, blind, doorless and windowless corridor of pain was waiting to open up and shut her in again.[16]

It is no surprise that a generation of women felt that, even in this most feminine of activities, their agency had been taken away with sedatives, knives and medieval-looking medical instruments. They did not want to have their babies removed from them like a malignant organ, wrapped and taken off to scream among rows of newborns in a sprawling, strip-lit hospital room. They didn't want to knock their children unconscious with litres of factory-processed feed and leave them to cry behind the high metal bars of their cots until they learned not to make a sound.

But the corrective of home-birth followed by two years of breastfeeding and five years of attachment parenting before school has inevitably become the preserve of the very wealthy. It is not possible for the 75 per cent of mothers who have to go back to a job.[17] It is not possible for the 15 per cent of families being brought up by a single parent.[18] Not to mention the 12 to 15 per cent of women who simply can't make enough milk to breastfeed their babies.[19]

The shift away from a male-dominated, highly industrialised and highly medicalised approach to childcare has
doubtless been of huge benefit to millions of mothers and
children. But most mothers have to find ways of balancing
those demands with the realities of their lives. They give birth
in the birthing centre rather than the hospital room, supported
by their husband, their wife or friend. They breastfeed for six
months, perhaps, maybe a year. They work part time.

This should mean that mothers are winning. But instead
they are trying to strike a balance in the face of incessant criticism and crippling guilt.

On the one hand, women are being let down by a
misogynistic medicalised obstetric culture. My mother
was a champion breastfeeder, but has always felt her three
Caesareans meant that she somehow failed at birth. And this
isn't paranoia. When she tried to give birth to me 'naturally',
having had a Caesarean for my brother, her old Caesarean scar
began to rupture. After a terrifying emergency Caesarean,
during which she almost died, she was wheeled back to the
ward where she caught sight of her notes. They read: 'Trial of
scar: Failed'.

Equally, there are millions of women who feel oppressed
by the demand that they should be some sort of lactating
earth goddess. Two women in my family had 'natural' births
but were pushed to breastfeed despite not being able to make
enough milk to feed their babies. Their midwives were constantly telling them that everyone can breastfeed, quoting an
outdated but oft-used statistic from the US that only 1 per
cent of women are actually unable to breastfeed, when the
real figure is up to fifteen times higher.[20] In both cases, their
doctors had to intervene when their babies weren't putting on
weight. Both were deeply traumatised by being told by one
medical professional that they had been starving their baby

and by another that they could have breastfed if they'd just tried hard enough.

Not a single woman in my family came anywhere close to the ideal of the home-birthing, breastfeeding, attached mother and at times each of them was made to feel terrible about it. Despite the fact that their children were and are happy and healthy.

I am not advocating that these women should not have been encouraged to breastfeed. But why couldn't it have been encouragement? What would have been so wrong about saying to a woman struggling to breastfeed: do your best. If we don't crack it, then it's not the end of the world.

And let's not forget that these are white, middle-class women having children in some of the world's richest nations. If they don't have the resources to fulfil the mothering standards expected of them, then who does?

All of these impossible benchmarks should have been easy for my husband and I to ignore. We adopted. We are two dads. We did not give birth. We could not have breastfed. And yet, for us – as for other adoptive parents, parents who can't breastfeed, whose children require serious medical interventions the moment they are born – this obsession with what is 'natural' and 'traditional' for our child feels like a constant attack. It is a minefield that is simply impossible to traverse without feeling like you're about to be blown sky high.

When we met our son for the first time the foster carer who'd looked after him for the first four weeks of his life told us that she fed him with a milk powder called Babyvita. When the midwife visited us on our first day at home with our son she shook her head in indignation when we showed her the box.

'Nestlé Beba Pre is the only thing you should be giving your son. It's the most tested.'

Every time we took our tin of Nestlé milk powder off the shelf in the drugstore we were greeted with a giant sticker telling us that our child should be being breastfed. We felt like we were poisoning him.

'Not the organic one?' a visiting friend said when they saw the tin on the shelf.

'I always think babies need a breast,' said a guest at a wedding we went to. 'But he seems OK, I suppose.'

Another said, 'Maybe he won't be susceptible to asthma. You might get lucky. Though I suppose you never know if they're adopted.'

'Nestlé?' said a friend without kids. 'You know they're basically evil.'

The doctor said, 'Just don't chop and change. Once you're on one, stick with it.'

After a year of bottle-feeding, we pushed our trolley into the baby section of the drugstore and found a recall label on the Beba Pre saying that traces of mineral oil had been found in some tins of Nestlé milk and they were temporarily out of stock.[21]

Sometimes still, a few minutes after we've turned the light off, my husband will say: 'I do still worry about that baby milk. I really regret it.' And I have to hold his hand in the dark and tell him we did our best.

## Joy

There are no winners in our current version of the 'traditional' family. A few companies, perhaps, a few medical professionals. But certainly not mums and dads and their children.

When I talk about mothers being genuinely able to choose equitable parenting, I'm not talking about women who want to look after their children full time being told they can't. I'm not talking about parents assiduously dividing up parenting fifty-fifty and berating each other for failing to keep their side of the bargain. What I'm talking about is a society in which any woman who wants to have a child has as much say about how childcare is going to be divided up as her husband or partner. I am talking about women genuinely having the opportunity to parent in a way that suits them and their partner best. Not their doctor. Not their own parents. Not their peers or their midwife or their employer. I am talking about women being allowed to have the parenting experience that, for the most part, my husband and I have been allowed to have.

As I say, this kind of parenting would not just be a win for Mum. It's a win for everyone involved in this relationship. There are decades of evidence suggesting that the more engaged both parents are with their children, the more secure their children will be, the higher their IQ, even. The more quality time a child's father spends with them, the less likely it is that their child will drop out of school, go to prison or even engage in risky sexual behaviour as a teenager.[22]

And what about fathers? There is plenty of evidence that men are also losing out in the traditional family model and that there are both mental and physical benefits to engaged fatherhood.[23]

But the real benefits of shared parenthood for men are much harder to sum up. When I went back to work after my parental leave, I bumped into a friend on the train to work who has four kids. When he asked me how the first year had been, I ended up telling him about our lack of sleep, the relentlessness of childcare, related a list of funny stories about being vomited on, peed on, shat on. As the train pulled into his stop, I had to desperately throw in, 'It's been great, though.'

'It's funny, isn't it,' my colleague said from the train door.

'The trouble is, parenting always sounds like a nightmare, because it's so easy to talk about the bad things that happen. But so impossible to sum up what's good about being a dad.'

He was so right. But here's my best shot.

As I touched on at the beginning of this chapter, I feel less anxious about myself since my son arrived. I have always been an anxious person. I have struggled with it throughout my life. As uncomfortable as it makes me to say it, there is a certain narcissism inherent to anxiety. Your concern, usually, is for yourself. This particular kind of anxiety has been kicked into focus for me by parenthood.

I feel genuinely rooted in the world. I feel like I have a hand in the game. That can be anxiety-provoking, of course, but there is no question that I have become more empathetic and not just in terms of other parents. I am more responsive to other people's stories. I feel books, films, music more deeply. I am much more forgiving of other people's mistakes. I am more wary of saying something mean about someone behind their back to get a laugh.

There is an incredible expansiveness of experience about being a dad. I always loved being at home. Cabin fever holds little fear for me. I didn't understand my parents' upset when I watched TV on a sunny day; I don't understand it now – the sunny day doesn't care if I don't grace it with my presence. This has its advantages, but it has also meant that I have a tendency, especially as a writer, to allow my world to get quite small.

Fatherhood means I have to leave the house every day. Fatherhood means that I have to deal with the gamut of human emotion on a second-by-second basis. I have to wander through town covered in ice cream, sand and snot. I have to endure the knowing stares of supermarket customers when my son appears to be saying I don't feed him and appears to be screaming for his 'Papa' – a name that apparently doesn't refer to me. I have to deal with being pushed and pushed until I snap at him and then deal with the guilt of snapping. And then the simultaneous worry that I'm both a soft touch and an authoritarian father.

All of these challenges push at the borders of my experience and make the world seem like a much less strange, less scary place.

Then there's joy.

I was prepared for the challenges, even if I couldn't quite comprehend how they were going to feel. The joy has been the surprise. I have just enjoyed being a parent much more than I had expected to. I had somehow thought that the pleasure of parenthood would be a sort of ascetic sense of goodness. But it's just fun. The three of us are all just having the best time.

# Real Parents

## The Adoption Problem

Before we adopted, my major worry was how Tom and I would be judged in public. Would people stare at us?* Would they shout at us? Would they refuse to serve us or laugh at us?

As I've outlined above, there have been odd reactions. But it turns out, in fact, that, even when you're splitting up childcare relatively evenly, public parenthood, certainly during the working week, is quite a lonely business. For five days of the week one of you is working and the other one is on their own with the kid; and when you're all together in the evening you're at home. There are moments when we're out that people clock us as a threesome, but on most days, aswim in the daily soup, it is not hard to forget that our family is not like other families.

---

* Germans in general, and Berliners in particular, have a very different relationship to staring. If someone's staring at you in the UK, you only have to meet their gaze to send their eyes swiftly groundwards. Not in Berlin. If a Berliner is interested in what you're wearing, what you're reading, how your family is constituted, they will happily stare at you while they consider this, whether you stare back or not. The same is true generally of personal space. I was once gently but firmly pushed into an open freezer cabinet in the supermarket. The Berliner in question was silent, while I kept saying, 'Oh excuse me. Oh I am sorry,' as my face was slowly squashed into a packet of frozen peas.

When it comes to our son's adoption, my expectations were reversed. I had expected almost no reaction. But the reactions have been strong and, to me, surprising.

I've known a few people who were adopted. My husband's family includes people who were both adopted and fostered. Both he and I grew up with adopted friends; one of my first childhood pals, Will, was adopted. Will's adoption was something we all knew about at school, but it didn't seem much more important to us than the fact that his mum was a teacher or that he was much younger than his two older siblings. They were all just things we knew about Will.

As a child, you take the world at face value in whatever way it is presented to you. I was interested in Will's adoption; I remember asking him if he knew who his biological parents were – as a child I probably said 'real parents' – but Will seemed unfazed. He just told me what he knew about them and we went back to hammering the keys of our Acorn Electron.

I thought that people were going to feel the same way about our son. But in fact we have had as many odd reactions to him being adopted as we've had to him having two dads. And we've had some pretty odd reactions to that.

'Oh, how gorgeous,' one colleague said to me when I showed her a picture of our son on my phone. 'I suppose you must love him like he was a normal child.'

This comment, which I've heard in a number of different guises, is, I think, one of the hardest to respond to.

One response might be, 'What's a "normal" child?' Another might be, 'I have no comparison, but I can't imagine loving him more, so I suppose so.' But really, I want to say, 'What the fuck do you think you're talking about?'

I don't say that, though. I say: 'Of course. And he is a normal child.'

'Oh sure,' they respond with a comforting, tight-lipped smile and nod that suggests 'And isn't it sweet that you think so'.

Another friend texted me a picture of their daughter and wrote: 'I only started to really feel love for her when she started to look like me.'

At least when such a message comes in the form of a text you can mutter 'Are you fucking kidding me?' as you text them back a heart emoji.

Like the solicitor who did our adoption, these are nice people. These are the sort of things that good people say to us, people who aren't trying to be malicious. And I think they would be appalled to find out that they'd upset us. But these comments do betray their thinking and it is hard to be forgiving of that.

It's a bit like the husband of one of my female friends who always calls me 'John', which is the name of his wife's other gay friend. He's always very apologetic every time I point it out and I never get openly angry with him. But it makes me sad, nevertheless, to get so clear an insight into which pen in his brain he has rounded me up.

## The Invention of Western Adoption

Adoption is often assumed to be akin to marriage: an essential and ancient point of family law that is universally understood. In fact, what we in the West generally understand as the archetypical adoption – a couple who can't have children adopting the child of someone they don't know – is a relatively new and highly Western notion.

If we define adoption at its most basic, as a parent raising a child that is not biologically their own, then adoption is indeed as natural as birth. In the animal kingdom, elephants, monkeys, dogs, rodents, birds and social insects all commonly adopt the offspring of other parents and bring them up as their own. More surprising and more moving still, zoologists have failed to come up with a clear evolutionary reason for adoption; adopting a baby elephant from another female elephant does not particularly benefit the adopting parent. The current consensus is that these relationships are instinctively altruistic. That is to say, a chimpanzee that adopts the orphan child of another chimpanzee does it out of an instinct for the infant's good and not their own.[1]

Adoption as a legal framework for defining new parent–child relationships appears in the Code of Hammurabi, a set of laws gathered together in 1772 BC and the oldest major legal text currently known.[2] Over the following centuries, laws on adoption were codified in Ancient Egypt, in Ancient Greece and Rome.

Many of our foundational stories are stories of adoption. The story of Exodus, of Moses found by Bithiah, daughter of the Pharaoh, on the banks of the Nile, is a story of adoption. The story of Oedipus, spared death when he was spirited away from his house by a servant, is a story of adoption. The story of Midas too begins with Dionysus, god of wine, going in search of his foster father Silenus and rewarding the misguided Midas with his choice of compensation for returning his father to him.

Adoption was common in Ancient China and it was practised in all regions and among all classes in pre-Raj India.[3] Adoption in the Middle East is mentioned in the Bible, although, in Western Europe, the legality of adoption was suppressed from the fifth century onwards. Because propertied men without heirs generally left their money to the Catholic Church, it became profitable for the Church to undermine adoption as 'unnatural'. This required contemporary theologians to recast the many positive Biblical references to adoption ('For ye have not received the spirit of bondage again to fear; but ye have received the Spirit of adoption, whereby we cry, Abba, Father'),[4] which were palmed off as metaphorical.[5]

Until the Industrial Revolution, adoption in the upper echelons of European society was tied up in issues around legitimacy and inheritance. Among the agricultural workers that made up the bulk of the population, orphaned and abandoned children were usually raised informally in their extended families. The shame of illegitimate birth combined with the high incidence of infectious diseases and women dying in childbirth made it a relatively regular occurrence. Indeed, the very first English novels commonly focused on foundlings like Tom Jones and Moll Flanders, brought up in ad hoc parental arrangements.

The explosive industrial growth that began in England during the nineteenth century led to an increasingly mobile working population, with more children being born far away from their extended families. This in turn led to the growth of so-called 'baby farms' in which labouring mothers paid a stipend to have their baby raised by private 'baby farmers', like the gloriously despicable Mrs Sucksby in Sarah Waters' *Fingersmith*.[6] These children were often abandoned, malnourished and maltreated, and because the arrangement was illegal the children's mothers had no recourse to have the baby farmers prosecuted.[7]

In the United States, the story of formal adoption agreements began with white settlers adopting the children of Native American families. In these early agreements, the Native American families often understood that they were entering into an open exchange of kinship and stopped actively participating in the practice when they realised it was irrevocable. Native American children 'adopted' there-after were in fact forcibly removed to be 'civilised' and 'Americanised' in Christian boarding schools.[8]

In Britain, scandals, including baby farming and the explosion of orphaned children in industrial cities, drove philanthropists like Thomas Bowman Stephenson and Dr Barnardo to set up homes for destitute, orphaned children and to push for the legal formalisation of adoption.[9] As the United States began to industrialise in turn, the waves of migrant Europeans arriving in the country led to its own orphan crisis, which church groups such as the Children's Aid Society of New York tried to address by putting children on 'orphan trains' to the West to work as farm hands and, in some cases, be formally adopted by new families.[10]

But it was not until the beginning of the twentieth century, when lower infant mortality rates and access to early forms of contraception allowed more affluent women to have fewer children and thus the capacity to adopt, that the first modern adoption legislation was passed. In the UK, this was in the form of the 1926 Adoption of Children Act.[11] In the United States, a federal framework for adoption was first put in place during the 1930s.

The great majority of American children put up for adoption during this time came from the maternity home movement in which unmarried middle-class white women were able to give birth to illegitimate children in secret who were then adopted by other white middle-class families who could not themselves conceive.

Although this offered a solution to the problem of ille-gitimate pregnancies at a time when there was a great social stigma attached to giving birth out of wedlock, many mothers felt that they had little choice in giving up their children. This issue was particularly acute in countries with strict abortion laws and strong religious sensibilities; in Ireland during the 1960s, 97 per cent of children born to unwed mothers were put up for adoption.[12]

When we talk about the archetype of adoption in the West, it is this kind of adoption that we are talking about. A mother cannot keep her child for social or personal reasons, she gives it up in secret, and that child is raised by another family. When we discuss modern developments in our thinking around adoption, we are defining them against this 'traditional' model. And yet this kind of adoption only existed in this form for about fifty years and only really affected white women. Women of colour were shut out of the adoption process in the West as prospective adopters and the children of their unwed sons and daughters were usually raised informally within the wider family.[13]

Over the course of the last century, in Europe, North America and Australasia, the legal framework for adoption and public attitudes towards it changed significantly. Despite the new adoption laws put into place during the 1930s and 1940s, informal adoptions were still common in pre-war Europe with thousands of children never knowing that the parents raising them were not their biological parents. The structure of adoption was increasingly formalised to deal with these issues, but it was still common practice in the West up until the 1980s to keep children's adoption a secret. Indeed, children, such as the writer Jeanette Winterson, who were adopted before 1976 went through sealed adoptions that promised both the child and birth parents anonymity, often making it impossible for adopted children to locate their birth parents as adults.[14]

The high point of American adoption occurred in 1970 when 175,000 children were adopted.[15] In England and Wales, the peak of adoptions occurred in 1968 when 24,831 adoption orders were issued. It was the year after the introduction of the contraceptive pill, but still a time in which most unmarried mothers felt unable to raise their children alone.[16]

This was as much about the practicalities of single parenthood as the moral condemnation that single mothers still faced. Outside the upper middle classes, few young women wanting to forge a life for themselves and their child had received enough formal education to take up well-paid skilled work. In the UK, it wasn't until the late 1970s that unmarried women were even allowed to apply for council housing without a husband.[17]

The 1970s also saw an increase in parents from Western countries adopting internationally – a project that was initially framed in terms of white North American, European and Antipodean parents 'rescuing' children from what were then considered developing countries like China, South Korea and India. This wave was also brief. The crest formed around 2004 when 22,986 international adoptions took place in the USA alone[18] and international adoption was widely covered in the press when celebrities like Madonna and Angelina Jolie began adopting from Vietnam, Cambodia and Malawi.[19]

As the first internationally adopted children came of age and began to research their backgrounds, they uncovered widespread corruption and bribery.[20] This led to many countries shutting down what had in effect become people-trafficking businesses run by 'a bureaucracy of adoption agencies with a vested interest, both monetary and social, in making children "adoptable" for prospective adoptive parents'.[21] The effect of these countries closing their adoption industries was that, by 2019, just 2,971 children were adopted in the USA from outside its national borders – an almost 90 per cent drop in just fifteen years.[22]

But it isn't just international adoption that has seen a rapid decline. The sexual revolution, the falling birth rate across the Western world, the increasing number of women who felt able to raise their children outside marriage – all of these factors led to a steady downturn in the number of children being put up for adoption in Europe and North America.

The great adoptive century ended with an increasing number of fertility options available to parents who couldn't conceive naturally, which eroded the number of parents considering adoption as a way to start a family. In the USA, adoption numbers have fallen from their peak of 175,000 to around 140,000, a drop of 20 per cent.[23] The slump in adoptions in European countries has been much more dramatic. By 2020, just 3,440 adoption orders were issued in England and Wales – just 7 per cent of the 1968 peak. In smaller European countries, from Norway to Greece, adoptions have dwindled to just a few hundred a year.[24]

The biggest change to approaches to adoption in the West over the last few decades is perhaps less about numbers and more about recognising the complexities of the relationship being formed. There is a big shift towards openness in the adoption process, both in terms of sharing information with adopted children and, where possible, staying in touch with their birth parents. There is also a recognition of the complexities inherent in a process that always involves profound loss, however 'successful' a placement is.

We witnessed this generational shift first-hand during our adoption process. Our first social worker was in her sixties and was about to be seconded to another department. We were talking about what kind of language we might use about our prospective child's mother when he was old enough to talk about her.

'Our friends, who also adopted, use the term "tummy mummy",' Tom said.

The social worker winced and shook her head. 'No. I wouldn't use the term "mummy" at all. She's not the child's mother. She's not bringing them up. That's not a mother. It'll just confuse the child. I would just refer to them by their name – Jennifer, or whatever.'

We nodded, though it seemed quite a hard approach and didn't marry with what we'd heard from other adoptive parents.

Our social worker changed department three months into our process and our new social worker, who was about our age and was a few weeks into her first post, brought up the topic again.

'Well, Frau Welke said we shouldn't refer to her as a mother at all.'

The new social worker looked panicked. 'No, I think that would be a very bad idea. I mean, whatever the situation is, she carried them and gave birth to them. It's fine for your child to know that. In fact, it's vital. I'm sure that's not what Frau Welke said.'

'Maybe we misunderstood,' I said. We hadn't.

In international adoption too, adoptees now old enough to explore and tell their own stories are expressing the complex issues around being raised by well-meaning parents who wanted them to feel no different from anyone else, but in a world in which they were seen as other. 'For the Korean adoptees I spoke to,' the professor and adoptee Jessica Walton says in her book on American adoption from South Korea, 'this embodied experience of a white identity due to being racially and culturally socialised in white adoptive families is contested by the fact that they are not socially perceived as racially white, and instead become "Asian" through a "racialisation" of their bodies'.[25] These children were brought up to feel 'white' but still experienced the same racial intolerance, the same othering, that any Asian person in America or Europe experiences.

Although approaches to adoption in the past have failed to tackle the complexities of the experience of being adopted, my sense is that there is an exciting shift happening. It is a movement, led by adoptees – rather than adoption professionals and adoptive parents – to recognise and honour the intricacies of the adoptive experience.

The attempts by agencies, governments and adoptive parents to simplify the stories of children's adoptions – if they were revealed to them at all – did not make things easier for those children. It made things easier for the agencies, governments and parents. And the job of tackling the complexities and ambiguities of adoption was shifted to the child who faced a lifetime of coming to terms with their adoption, often on their own.

## Birth Parents

Considering that our son is being brought up by two dads, which you might assume would mean that we felt being a dad was as important as being a mother, not one person has ever asked us about our son's biological father.

'Do you have contact with his mother?' we get.

'It's so heartbreaking to imagine a mother giving up her child,' we hear.

But, to the people we meet, his biological father has no meaning; he is invisible, despite being responsible for half of our son's genetic make-up.

The reason, of course, is that, deep down, most people don't think that being a father matters as much as being a mother.

'A mother is important,' my husband's supervisor said to

him during his psychotherapy training, 'and a father becomes important.' I found this a bit insensitive at the time, and I find it pretty offensive now.

And yet, if I'm completely honest, I also think far more often about Theo's biological mother than his biological father. For me this is partly because, although she has not played any role in his upbringing, she did carry him and give birth to him. It moves me, often to tears, to think that her body is and will forever be changed by that experience. That whatever she does in her life, whatever she thinks about what happened to her, he will still be imprinted on her body at some deep biological level.

When I think about my son's biological father I am struck too by the fact that he is sitting somewhere now driving, drinking coffee, working through his emails. These two people who I don't really know make up the two halves of someone I know better than anyone else in the world. I don't have a relationship with them, and yet I am completely in love with the coalescence of their genes.

We all want the world to be more simple than it is. Friends say to us, 'You should be glad you don't have any contact with his parents. The stories you hear.' They simultaneously want to know about my son's 'real' parents, while wanting them to be invisible. 'You're all that matters now,' they say.

My son is a wonderful person. He is bright and genuinely friendly. He is sociable, curious, very charming. Unlike me, he is emotionally incredibly well balanced and has been since he was a baby. He does lose his temper, but never for long. He does cry when he's hurt himself, but rarely for attention. I of course think he's very beautiful; perfect, in fact. These wonderful traits of his were obvious the day we met him when he was just a few weeks old. They are not the result of our fine parenting.

I don't mean to say that we have had no influence on him. Every word he has spoken, every meal he has eaten, every expression he made sense of in his first two years of life came from us. But the foundations of his wonderful person were all already in place when we met him.

In the unlikely event that my son turns out to have absolutely no interest in his adoption story and never thinks about his birth parents, they will still always be essential because they were the root of everything that is good in him.

## Trauma

I have an issue with the increasing focus, in debates around adoption, on trauma. And it's not a reasonable one. My issue is that I look at my perfect little son toddling around our flat and I feel like the trauma of his adoption is something that we have to gift him.

It's not that I didn't think we would have to talk to him about trauma; in fact it is one of the main things you talk about during the adoption process and concomitant adoption preparation classes. We talked in endless detail about the thousands of psychological, physical and chemical experiences a child might face before adoption, each one subtly influencing their behaviour and emotions for years to come, if not their whole lives.

But then our imaginary child became a real son. A little boy who sleeps well, eats well, is thoughtful and happy and well adjusted. A boy whose main foci in life are toy cars, making tents out of blankets, ice cream, croissants and endlessly dancing to the Pippi Longstocking theme tune played on our mobile phones.

He does not wake up screaming in the night. His weight

and height are completely average. He speaks well. He has reached all of his developmental milestones. He is like any of his friends in nursery – except for this sad fact about his birth that we have to slowly make him aware of.

When we brought him home we constantly witnessed people reading his behaviour through the minimal information they knew about his past.

'You can see in his face that he's already experienced so much,' said a friend. We looked at Theo. He was asleep in his pram and looked, to us, much like any other baby.

That's not quite true. There was in fact one difference we noticed: his head was a little flat on one side. Our paediatrician was unconcerned – it often happens during birth, apparently, and evens out as the baby rapidly grows during the first year or two. But she said if we were worried we could take him to a paediatric physiotherapist who could check he was moving his head properly. The physiotherapist was also unconcerned about the flat side of his head, but suggested that he come for regular physiotherapeutic treatment anyway.

'Why?' asked Tom.

'He doesn't pass objects very quickly from one hand to the other. It could be to do with the trauma of his adoption.'

'In what way?'

'Well, these things always leave traces.'

'And normally a child would be passing objects from one hand to the other at three months old?'

'I mean, not always.'

'So it's not actually abnormal?'

'No. But some children can already do it.'

When Tom relayed this story back to me at home, I asked: 'So what does he actually need physiotherapy for?'

Tom shrugged. 'That was a bit unclear. I think he's probably fine.'

Of course, if the question of what is genetic, what is trauma and what is upbringing is a complex one for the adoptive parent, it is a far more complex one for the adopted child. There is not just the question of whether this thought or that feeling has something to do with their adoption, but also of which parts of their personality are from their biological parents and which from their adoptive parents, which are a mixture of both or their very own.

As is the case with many adopted children, these questions took on a new prominence and poignancy for the writer Matthew Salesses when he himself had children:

> When I was a child, I used to get so lost in my thoughts that I couldn't hear anything else. I actually couldn't hear. I used to see words as pictures. I would read a book and it would be like watching a movie. If you said the name of a character to me, it would bring up a face, not a story.
>
> Maybe this has nothing to do with adoption. Or maybe everything has everything to do with adoption. This is the question I am never and can never be sure about. It is the question my baby is helping to answer, in part. The question who am I? Isn't that what we're always endlessly asking?[26]

I had initially felt judgemental about the parents we met during our adoption process who seemed to be afraid of their future children's trauma. There was a small group of straight couples for whom adoption was the last step in a very long journey to try and establish a family. These couples' questions betrayed a desire to be reassured that the child they might adopt was going to be like the child they had held in their imagination for ten or twenty years.

They would wince when another handout was passed around about the developmental effects of alcohol and drugs on prenatal babies. They would frown through films in which grown-up adoptees described the sadness they felt about being abandoned by their mothers. And after a presentation on the effects of neglect on small children they would ask:

'Are there any children who come from mothers who don't have any problems?'

'No,' the course leader would say. 'If the mothers didn't have any problems they wouldn't be giving up their babies for adoption.'

The parents frowned thoughtfully at this. After the course leader talked about her two children's very different reactions to being adopted, another mother said:

'What percentage of children are affected by being adopted?'

'One hundred per cent,' the course leader replied.

They winced again.

But now I wince just like those mothers winced when I pick up a book like *The Primal Wound* in which the psychologist and adoptive parent Nancy Newton Verrier suggests that one cannot 'replace the biological mother with another "primary caregiver" without the child being both aware of the substitution and traumatised by it'.[27]

It's not that I want a perfect family. The great advantage of being a gay adoptive parent is that, from a social point of view, your family is never going to reflect the perfect nuclear family, so most of the time you don't worry about it. It's just that I look at my beautiful son and can't bear the idea that something that happened to him in the first few days of his life, which had nothing to do with who he is, is going to define him, is going to make his life harder than it would otherwise be.

There are a number of homologues to an adopted child growing up without contact with one or both of their biological parents and each of these situations is understood completely differently. Most common is the huge number of children who grow up without any contact with just one of their parents, usually their biological father. In the UK, 10 per cent of all fathers – about a million dads – don't live with their children,[28] and 13 per cent of these – that's 130,000 dads – have no contact with their children. There is little research on how many children living with their fathers are estranged from their biological mothers, although, as adults, the figure is similar: a study in the United States suggests that about 10 per cent of adults have no contact with their biological mothers.[29]

Then there's surrogacy. Sperm donation and egg donation. In all of these cases, children are being born and are growing up without any connection to one of their biological parents and/or the woman who carried them.

Logically I understand that the psychological effect of your biological mother choosing to donate an egg is not the same as your biological mother giving birth to you and then giving you up. But in my irrational moments, when I'm desperately trying to map a path through the world for my son on which he will experience no pain, no fear and no rejection, I think: Why aren't these kids obliged to be traumatised? Why does my son have to deal with this shit and not them?

Approaches to adoption during the second half of the last century offer a few answers to that question. As we touched on when we talked about the history of adoption, post-war adoptions were often marked by generally well-meaning parents hoping to deal with their children's potential trauma by not telling them they were adopted at all. And when children were told, they were encouraged to think about themselves as no different from any other child.

The trouble was, that's not how the world perceived them. Biological children are not asked why they were adopted.

They are not questioned about where their 'real' parents are. They are not constantly told how lucky they are to have been adopted in the first place.

This difference is even more marked in intercultural and intercountry adoptions. During the heyday of international adoptions into Western countries, the overriding narrative was one of salvation — the poor foreign children being rescued from the Third World by white parents 'called to adoption' because it was 'in their hearts' to help orphans in need.[30]

But, as the writer and artist Lisa Wool-Rim Sjöblom so beautifully illustrates in her graphic memoir *Palimpsest*, being told that you are no different from any of your Swedish class-mates becomes a problem when you are treated completely differently from your Swedish classmates:

It took me over 30 years to just accept the fact that I'm Asian. I finally feel comfortable with that. I don't feel disappointed when I see myself in a mirror, or I feel dis-appointed, but on my own terms. But I don't feel anymore that I wish I was blond, or that I wish I had blue eyes. I can acknowledge a lot of things that I had just been pushing down in my desperate need to fit into all these narratives about what I'm supposed to be as an adoptee.[31]

What upsets me about these debates around adoption and trauma is perfectly captured in that final line: 'my desperate need to fit into all these narratives about what I'm supposed to be as an adoptee'.

I worry that, in focusing on our son's adoption as his ur-trauma, we are simply replacing one highly emotive narrative about how he is meant to feel about being adopted with another one. I completely agree with writers like Newton Verrier that it is no longer appropriate, indeed damaging, to say to an adopted child: the fact you are adopted doesn't mean anything and you are the same as any other child. But is it any better to say to a child: your adoption is a trauma that will mark you for the rest of your life? This is not a rhetorical question: I genuinely don't know. But as Matthew Salesses says: 'Adoption has always been more a question than an answer.'[32]

The gift – the impossible gift – that I would like to give my son is to offer him the facts of his adoption in a kind of social vacuum, a place without social pressures in which he can decide what being adopted means for him before someone else tells him what it means. Of course, that vacuum doesn't exist. On his second day of nursery, when he was two years old, another boy came up to us and said, 'Where's Theo's mum?'

'Theo has two dads,' I said.

'There's no such thing,' he said.

We had made it twenty-four hours in the real world.


## Two Dads

In the odd, rain-filled May of 2021, when, between showers, the air was filled with wispy plane-tree seedlings and the smell of lime blossom, we met up with another couple in Berlin who have an adopted son one year older than Theo.

The coronavirus was first identified when Theo had just turned one. For Tom and me, our year of parental leave bled straight into the pandemic. At home with our son, trying desperately to catch up with other commitments during his nap time, pandemic life was just an extension of the parental-leave life we had been living since he had arrived. But the lockdown wiped out nearly all social activities with Theo and other children. There were no toddler groups, no soft-play areas, no indoor swimming pools. We thus had little opportunity to meet up with other adoptive parents and swap stories.

What now struck me, as the mother started to talk about her three-year-old son, was how central his adoption was to their experience of parenthood. For them, it was the element of their family life that marked them out as different.

Of course, adoption has also been central to Tom and me becoming parents, but the difference is that, when we meet people, the first surprise is that Theo has two fathers. The problem that this adoptive mother saw in children's books was that they never talked about adopted children. The problem that we saw in children's books was that, not only did they almost never contain same-sex parents, they almost never contained dads.

We are delighted to find any picture book in which a father does any parenting, rather than just returning home at the end of the story to find a tiger has eaten all the food in the house. We are particularly pleased when we locate a book that shows a dad rather than a mum showing his child any kind of physical affection. We were distraught when *Hooray for Birds!*, our son's favourite Lucy Cousins book, fell to bits after a thousand readings and we purchased a new edition only to find that the ending had been changed from two genderless birds 'Cuddling together' to the baby bird 'Cuddling with mum' in order to create a new rhyme with 'wiggle your bum'.

We don't yet know what our son is going to think about having two dads, if he thinks about it at all. But my hope is that having two dads will actually make our son feel less of an odd-one-out, because his being adopted is not the main thing that makes our family different from other families. He is not the singularity in an otherwise average straight family. He is a unique part among unique parts in a unique set-up.

As a gay parent, you also have dealt with, if not the same

issues as your adopted child, then certainly related issues. You know what it's like to carry with you an identifier that means lots of very nuanced and complex things to you, but which the world at large sees in very simple terms – terms they are not very interested in having challenged. You know what it feels like to be told how you're meant to think and feel about who you are and how difficult that is to square with who you actually are. You know what it feels like to be seen as a type of person rather than just a person and sometimes to be liked and disliked for what you represent rather than who you are. You know how disheartening it is when people expect you to be grateful for things they take for granted. You know what it feels like to have, in one part of your life, a profoundly different social and emotional experience from everyone else in your family.

These are hopes, though. It may well be wishful thinking. Because however many books I read or doctors I talk to, the person who's going to tell us what it's like to be an adopted child with two dads like us is our son.

There is perhaps one final positive about being forced to think about your child's trauma before they experience it. And that is that it better prepares you for what all parents have to face: the fact that, however hard you try, your child is going to hurt. You wield so much power as a parent, but you don't have enough power to change that. The best you can hope for your child, the very happiest life you could imagine for them, is still going to be filled with moments of heartbreak, loneliness, fear and desperation. It is the worst thing about being a parent: that you can't save them from it all.

But that thought can also free you. Parenting can never be perfected. We all just have to try our best. Being a father to a child who's been through adoption gives you the privilege of starting parenthood in the full knowledge that nothing is ever going to be just right. That your joy is always going to be built on loss. That love, necessarily, is always going to be tempered by pain.

# Childlessness

## Old Parents

When I went to university I met, for the first time, people who had grown up in London. They seemed impossibly glamorous to me.

They wore interesting clothes I had never seen before. In 1990s Oxford, if you were under thirty you could only buy clothes from Topshop or Burton. You had seen all the clothes. If you bought a jumper, three other people in the sixth form would have that same jumper and you would catch up in advance of school photos and class trips to make sure you wouldn't be dressed the same.

I had anecdotes about throwing up in fields and drink-driving. These Londoners had never learned to drive. They had thrown up outside kebab shops, on the Underground and in clubs. And these clubs were not carpeted nor were they attached to bowling alleys off the M4. The clubs these Londoners had thrown up in did not have a 'no pumps or trainers' rule. They played hip-hop and dubstep; no one was cheering through the dry ice with their glow sticks when 'Sandstorm' came on for the third time.

Their anecdotes were about friends called Molly, Zaina and Ty. My anecdotes were about the four other Bens in my class or one of the three Sarahs from my village.

'Where are you from?' one of these Londoners said to me. He was very tall, openly gay at a time when I was not, and dressed all in white like a Backstreet Boy.

'A village near Oxford,' I said.

'The countryside?'

'Well, yeah,' I said, although I had never really thought of our village as properly rural because it had a post office.

He laughed. 'What, you have a Labrador, wellies and a Land Rover?'

I laughed. 'I mean, we have a West Highland Terrier too,' I said eventually. 'It's not just the Labrador. And you need wellies, because of the mud. And my *mum* doesn't drive a Land Rover.'

He nodded and pretended to inspect something on his pristine cargo trousers before slipping off down the corridor.

It was 1998 and, as well as espresso machines in their dorm rooms, these Londoners all had mobile phones. I had just got a pager for free in return for opening a student bank account with NatWest. I did have a number – a BT pager number, which I gave out to friends and family on a little card. They could call the number and relate a message to an operator who typed it into a computer. This message would then be sent to my pager, which would slowly reveal the text on a narrow screen, like those digital ticker tapes that display a constant stream of stock-market prices on Times Square.

I was very proud of my pager and carried it about with me religiously. But the only person who really used it was my mum. She would send me a message while I was on the train back home telling me, for instance, that she couldn't pick me up from Didcot Station. I was able to respond two hours later when I arrived at Didcot Station and finally had access to a payphone.

But what had really marked these Londoners out was how old their parents were.

In our village, having children in your thirties was considered pretty ancient. I did have primary school friends whose parents were in their forties, but these were what were referred to – openly and in their presence – as 'afterthoughts'.

My friend Nile was an afterthought. He used to come and 'call on me' and we would go to his house to carry out 'experiments', which generally meant covering Fiendish Feet yoghurt pots in super glue and setting them on fire. I considered his parents to be in their mid-seventies, but since his mother had given birth to him they can't have been older than fifty.

Their home was the home of the retiree. It was a bungalow with soft, grey carpets. They had separate beds with hard, high headboards, dark as pews. His grey-haired mother sat on a kneeling chair in front of her sewing machine. His bald father carved things in the shed. It was very clear to me that they had had him at the wrong age.

But my new London friends at university were not afterthoughts. They were the eldest children or only children of parents who had started thinking about having babies at thirty-five after a long and profitable career in jazz.

Of course, because I didn't imagine that I'd be having children at all I didn't spend much time imagining how old I might be when I had them. Tom and I met when we were twenty-six and twenty-seven, our friends started having children when we were around thirty. We began exploring options at about the same time, but life and legislation bumped us along for a few more years until we finally got that phone call when I was thirty-eight and Tom thirty-nine.

My concern with being an older parent than my own

parents – they had had three kids by the time they were twenty-nine and thirty-one respectively – is all about the future. I am constantly totting up the years to work out how old we'll be when our son leaves school, graduates, has children of his own.

Though, I have to say that even this concern can be a consolation. When I read about some event in the future – say, that HS2 will be completed in 2032 – I imagine, with not a little sadness, my fifty-two-year-old self racing through Warwickshire, complaining that the seats are too hard. But then I think, Oh, but Theo will be fourteen – and that's a lovely thought. I can't wait to meet fourteen-year-old Theo.

The big advantage of senior parenthood, though, is that you have lived most of your adult life without children. This means, for a start, that you are very aware that life changes, whether you have children or not. Friends who had children in their twenties had to struggle with their child-free friends partying on and living lives that constantly reflected back to them the life they might be living had they not reproduced. If you're in your late thirties, though, you know that the party stops anyway. You know that your friendships change, that people move away, fall out with each other, die. You know that, in having children, whatever age you are, you are choosing to change your life very radically. But it is a choice about the kind of change you're going to experience, not whether or not you will experience profound change at all.

You have also seen friends parenting their children and have had some time to reflect on how you might want to do it. More importantly still, you have seen them make it through to the other side. Kinvara was my first friend to have a child; she was twenty-six. When she was lost in the existentially exhausting, vomit-filled nappy years and told me how physically overwhelming and relentless it was, I remember rubbing her shoulder and saying that it was going to be all right, while all the time thinking: This is not going to be all right. I need to warn other women.

But now, when I see a picture of her heading out on the town with my teenage goddaughter, I know that whatever we think our current big challenge is with our son, it is going to be something completely different this time next year, something different again the year after that. I have seen so many friends paralysed with anxiety because of some injury or illness, tick* or developmental hurdle that, a few years later, they never even think about. I know that the challenges and consolations of parenthood are in constant flux and that whatever I find impossible today will be possible in the future.

But what twenty years of childless adulthood really teaches you is how challenging it is to live without children in a society that seems to be geared towards youthful excess for just ten years, before switching to family for the next fifty.

## The Line

We hated the line. It was a line used so often, when we didn't have kids, that it became like a drinking game prompt every time we visited our family or friends. At some moment during the weekend, when we protested about breakfast being scheduled for eight in the morning or asked whether a screaming child needed to be disciplined outside our bedroom door at three in the morning, it would be rattled out.

'You just can't understand. You don't have children.'

Why did I find this line so awful? Well, for a start, we had been talking to our friends and family for years about having

---

* Psychological or arachnid.

kids. Without having to know anything about our fertility, it was pretty clear that it was going to be much harder for us to have children than it had been for them. To me, it felt akin to saying to someone 'Well, you can't understand how stressful it is being rich' or 'You can't understand how limiting it is being beautiful'. The difference was that no one I knew – certainly no one I liked – would ever say any of those things to me. But plenty of people I liked and loved were happy to pull out 'the line' in times of stress.

It also smacked of martyrdom. As if parenthood were a suffering so appalling that no mere childless mortal could deign to fathom it.

This is, I think, related again to the great inequality in most people's parenting partnerships. If you're the mother, if you're completely overwhelmed and your husband can't understand what's so difficult about parenting, because he's barely doing any of it, then martyrdom is one of the few outlets left open to you. If you're always the one getting up at five in the morning, always the one dealing with every fever, every nappy and every plaster, then what other option do you have? Sometimes the only pleasure to be found in that unremitting responsibility is the sparse joy of suffering for the greater good.

But the ongoing inequality of parenthood is precisely why the sainthood–parenthood paradigm is such an issue. Parenthood is meant to be challenging. But it can still be more joyful or at least meaningful than it is challenging and over-whelming. If that's not the case for you, then you should be allowed to not have kids rather than be convinced that having kids, even though you know you're not going to enjoy it, is still a positive option for you.

I also hated the line because it set parents on a pedestal at a time when I wasn't a parent. Can one do anything more saintly than become a parent? Is there any state of being less criticisable? I feel like we let parents get away with anything and still they – and I now include myself in this – always push for more.

It is hard not to give in to the beautiful allure of parental power. When I get onto the train with my son and look about puppy-dog-eyed for a seat, people spring up to let me sit down. When I show people pictures of Theo on my phone, I see them glaze over after two, but I don't stop; I know they won't look away until I let them. When I tell my mum or dad another endearing story about my son's development, I can hear them flagging after the fourth such tale, but they chuckle away anyway when once they might have told me they had something on the stove.

When people see me with my son I mean something. I have social worth. I have a role people understand and they seem to be overjoyed by it. I feel completely included in the world. This is both a delight and a disappointment because I remember how it felt to be excluded. Childlessness rather than parenthood is still my normal state. Even if Theo leaves home at twenty, I will still have spent as much of my adult life being without children as being with them.

And yet, I don't see among my friends a correlation between how much parenthood changes you and how old you are when you become a parent. In the same way that alcohol suppresses and highlights qualities already existent within you, so too does parenthood work on desires, dislikes and anxieties you already had before you had children.

Parents constantly use their children to excuse the things they do and don't do. But what becomes apparent as an older dad, from two decades of observing other people parent, is that the things that people suddenly can't do because of their children are the things they didn't like doing before they had children.

We have friends you could never convince to leave their flat and now their children are the reason they can never leave the flat. We have friends who were always anxious at social gatherings and now their children are the reason they have to suddenly cancel plans. We have friends who, during weekends away, were always annoyed at how late everyone went to bed and how late they slept in the next day. Now their children are the reason that everyone has to be at the breakfast table at dawn.

The trick that used to annoy me most among my parent friends is what is known here in Germany as a Polish exit* – that is, leaving a party without saying goodbye. The parental version would involve one or sometimes both parents taking their children up to bed after dinner. Generally, these were the kind of parents who had developed an hour-long bedtime routine for their children. After an hour slowly bled into two it would become apparent that these parents were not coming back.

At one dinner party we went to, the father disappeared while the two-year-old he'd taken to bed returned to the party. The couple split up a few months later, thus I have never seen the man since he disappeared into that dusky bedroom doorway ten years ago.

I am not against hour-long bedtime routines nor even falling asleep while putting your child to bed. But what always annoyed me about these parents was that these things were rarely owned as choices.

Many people I know claim that their child cannot go to sleep unless one of their parents is lying next to them, stroking

---

* This term is found in most European languages in combination with whichever country the language traditionally denigrates. In English, it is, inevitably, either known as an Irish Goodbye or a French Exit. In French it is, of course, known as *filer à l'anglaise* – to leave English style. The English are in fact the culprits in most other countries, from Belgium and Poland to Hungary and the Czech Republic.

their foreheads for an hour until they drift off. There is, no doubt, some exceptional child for whom this is genuinely the case. But this is not a genetic or behavioural reality for most children. We know this, because we were once those children. And I wager that you also didn't have a single friend whose parents lay next to them for an hour until they fell asleep.* My parents were considered deeply lax because we had a night light.

I would love it if more parents felt able to express their parental choices as exactly that: choices. It would have made things much easier for me as a friend without children to hear them say: I know planning in an hour for our kid's bedtime means we can't all sit down to eat at 7.30, but it's really important to me.

It is for our friends and family, particularly those without kids, to say what annoying preferences my husband and I palm off as parental necessities. I would guess that Theo's napping would probably be one of them. Among what I obviously consider to be our boy's prodigious talents is his ability, aged three, to have a two- to three-hour nap in the afternoon and still go to bed at 8.30. He is now at an age where his friends are dropping their naps, but who wants to stop their child giving them a three-hour break every Saturday and Sunday? It means that we often can't do anything social in the early afternoon, and I hold my hands up and admit that that is my choice. Sorry, friends! I still love you.

*

---

If you wanted to defend the line, your best comeback would be the most simple. That the statement is true. There are simply lots of things you can't understand if you're not a parent.

I would concede the point. Although I think of myself as a pretty empathetic person, there were a thousand little moments in the company of family and friends when I watched parents feeding or disciplining their children and was baffled that they were so clearly getting it wrong. I would watch parents set boundaries and instantly break them, tell their children three times they couldn't eat the cake and then crack and give them the cake anyway, watch them discipline their children completely reasonably for bad behaviour and a minute later tearfully tell them they were 'a good boy'.

What I was failing to account for in these situations – the piece of the puzzle that was missing for me – was the crushing, subjugating power of parental love. I strongly feel that children should be given a broad range of nutritious foods, should be taught to eat at the table politely, should learn to love freshly prepared vegetables and challenging flavours. The problem is that I am desperate for my son to eat. And I'm desperate for him to be happy.

When he's ill and off his food, I feel his weight-loss physically. So even if we start at the table with wholegrain pasta, some roasted cauliflower and homemade tomato sauce, we will often end up on the sofa with me feeding him buttered white toast or yoghurt mixed with jam.

I read articles about how to surreptitiously hide vegetables in your children's meals, but I often do the opposite – frantically butter his peas and stir peanut butter into his porridge so that he won't waste away. He is not, I should add, wasting away. He is a completely normal-sized child. And yet there is a walnut of anxiety deep within me that drives me to try and fatten him up in case of emergency.

I desperately want to fully embrace the dietitian and psycho-therapist Ellyn Satter's advice to 'split the responsibility' – it is my responsibility to make the food; it is his responsibility to eat the food. I want to prepare my son some nutritious dhal and calmly return him to the table twenty times to eat it. But if he barely touches his food I can't help pulling anything edible from the fridge to push upon him, lying to him even just to get him to eat (I once told him quiche was a type of cake). Recently, after a particularly protracted round of presenting plate after plate of chopped peppers, scrambled eggs, toast, avocado slices and roasted chicken thighs, Theo pulled his bib off and ran away empty-stomached, leaving me to clear away what looked like a meze spread for a casual family brunch.

We break a million other rules of our own making. We bring him into our bed when he won't go back to sleep when we should be leaving him in his; we bark at him when he smashes something we've told him not to touch, then cuddle him the moment he starts crying; we tell him he can't take a toy car to bed then somehow find ourselves giving him three.

All of this I truly did not understand until I had kids.

But this does not let the line off the hook. Because the line is true of everything. Before I lived in Berlin I had a clear sense of what it would be like to live there. Some of it was accurate, much of it was not. This did not mean that I was shouting 'You can't understand, you don't live in Germany' to my friends and family every time they got upset that I wasn't coming to a birthday or a wedding.

'You can't understand, because you don't have children' is a cry of desperation. The line says, I am overwhelmed and I want you to leave me alone. And this feels so bad in this moment and I feel so emotional and it makes me furious that you can't feel that.

This is heartbreaking. But what the person without a child on the receiving end of the line hears is: you are of less worth than me because you have no child. The things that I am doing that are annoying you are so beyond your comprehension that there is no point in me even addressing your selfish needs. I am beyond criticism. I am selfless. You are a needy, childless narcissist who has no real problems.

I therefore make a plea to all parents never to tell anyone who doesn't have kids that they couldn't possibly understand what it's like to have kids. What you're trying to express matters, but it is coming across very differently from how you intend it to come across.

Although we don't hear the line any more, we have not been let off the hook. Recently, I called a friend who had pulled the line on us a few times over the years. Her husband had taken their eldest out for the day and she said to me, 'I'm so relaxed. I mean, there's almost nothing to do.' And then she said, '*Also, ein Kind ist kein Kind*,' which translates as something like 'Of course, one kid's as good as no kids'.

When I pointed out that that was a bit harsh, considering we had one kid, she said, 'Ben, please. You can't understand. You don't have two kids.'

## Jealousy

Much has been written about how men have to bear the loss of being demoted from being the number one person in their wife or partner's life to being the second most important. In his essay 'Man, Dying', the American writer Garth Stein describes sharing his marital bed with his son thus:

I am jealous of my son. In the night, he rolls around lux-
uriously in the bed, upside down, sideways, arms and legs
flopped every which way. He sleeps so soundly while I
struggle fitfully, clinging to the edge, trying not to resent
him. *I* should be the one burrowing my head into my wife's
mane of hair. *I* should be hugging her tightly around her
neck as he is. Matching her sleeping breaths, warming
myself to her body heat. Yet I cede this pleasure to him,
because he is my son.[1]

These are not sentiments I share for a range of reasons. For a
start, my husband's body and thus my relationship to it was not
changed by us having children. My husband wasn't pregnant.
His genitals and chest did not take on new meaning through
birth and breastfeeding. He did not have to deal with the radical emotional and physical changes of growing and birthing
a baby on his own, while I was left to massage his lower back.
The changes that he has experienced as a parent are the same
as the changes I have experienced.

This also means that, although we are different people and
take on different roles in our parenting, we still have the same
physical and emotional relationship to our son. There are
moments of favouritism when he wants to be comforted by one
of us more often than the other. But during those times when
our son is unwell or sleeping badly and we have to bring him
into our bed he is as interested in cuddling up to me as he is
in cuddling up to my husband.

Even when my husband puts our son's needs above my
needs, these are nearly always times when I would also put
my son's needs above my needs. In the same way that I have
never felt the straight mother's loss of identity as a parent, I
also cannot share the straight father's sense of jealousy.

I am not jealous because my relationship with my husband

seems so obviously different from my relationship with my son. When I watch my husband dress, feed and bathe our son, when I watch them cuddle, play and read together, I see a relationship like my relationship with my son, not like my relationship with my husband.

Part of the straight father's jealousy surely stems from the fact that there is something parental in their relationship with their wives. This is again fed by the traditional division of marital roles that still haunts most straight people's relationships. If, as a mother, you are cooking, laundering and cleaning for your children, you are also doing this for your husband. And your husband witnesses you enacting his mother's relationship to him. The same is happening when your wife witnesses you returning home from work, car keys in hand with your sleeves rolled up and the scent of office coffee and end-of-day sweat in your shirt. A combination that a number of straight female friends have told me really turns them on.

If you are in a straight relationship and this comparison makes you wince, I would ask you to reflect on how ingrained the language of parental relations is in mainstream romantic discourse. The most common nickname for our beloved is 'baby' and derivations thereof – 'baby girl', 'baby boy', 'my girl', 'bae'. A beautiful woman is a 'babe'. A hot guy might even be your 'daddy'. It is interesting to take a moment here to reflect on how keen straight society is to equate homosexuality with paedophilia and incest,[2] when the modern ideal of straight feminine beauty is a woman shaved of secondary sexual characteristics and the search terms 'mom', 'step-mom', 'MILF', 'step-sister' and 'teen' continue to grace the top ten most-searched terms on sites like PornHub.[3]

Far from empowering men, our current conceptions of 'traditional' marriage actually infantilise them. The single mother continues to be a maligned figure, but she is nevertheless a strong figure. The single mother copes.

The divorced father, on the other hand, the widowed husband, is a figure of pity, cut loose from the support he needs just to run his life, completely unable to survive alone. In William Maxwell's wonderful Spanish Flu novella *They Came Like Swallows*, the only response that the patriarch James Morison can fathom to the death of his wife is to wind up his whole family, apportioning the assets like an insolvent business:

> The best and possibly the only solution, so far as James could see, was for Clara to take the baby. And the boys, too. For he couldn't keep the house going – that was certain. He'd have to store what furniture he wanted. That wasn't much. He had never cared for antiques the way Elizabeth did. And sell all the rest. Sell the house, too, for what he could get.
>
> Wilfred had not offered to take the boys, but it would be all right, probably. James would give Clara so much a month for boarding them and for their clothes – because he would not have Wilfred or anybody else paying for the support of his children. And he'd get a room near by. Clara's wasn't the kind of home they were used to, perhaps. But it would do until such time as he was able to make a better arrangement.
>
> In the long run it was a mistake to have children. James did not understand them. He never knew what was going on in their minds. But that was Elizabeth's doing, after all. It was she who had wanted them.[4]

In our beloved nuclear family, the mother is, from conception to death, in constant transition. Pregnancy, motherhood, menopause. The child too. Sperm, embryo, foetus, baby then toddler, child then teenager, ward and then carer. Only the traditional father is in stasis. He ages slowly, but he experiences no shocking change. He keeps his job, he keeps his status, he keeps his friends and his interests and his habits. It is his fortune but also his tragedy.

He dismisses his wife's issues as 'women's issues' about which she is a little 'hysterical' – a word meaning 'of the womb', premised on the idea that the uteri of some women became detached and began to roam about their bodies, pushing at their throats and making them crazy. In fact, in becoming a mother and a primary carer, his wife is embarking on decades of extreme pain and loss.

Had James Morison died of the Spanish Flu, Elizabeth Morison would have been distraught, but would have kept her family together, would have carried on. She would have done it because she had done it before. When she lost her youth the day she gave birth. When she lost the body of her youth the day she became pregnant. When she gave birth and experienced a pain so unlike anything she had ever felt before that she understood how much pain a person might be expected to feel. When her children, to whom she had devoted her life, stopped loving and needing her in the way that they had once loved and needed her, believing that her love had changed too. But it was her only constant.

You will have seen powerful men in your own life fall apart in the face of change. Unemployment, retirement, bereavement leaving them completely lost. The widower has none of the cold strength of the widow. He is a boat set adrift, desperately searching for the shore.

The changes I have experienced as a father, despite not coming close to those of a mother, have nevertheless been profound. Being the primary caregiver to your child is a crash course in fear and loss, encircled in love.

The oft-quoted homologue to fathers' jealousy of their

children is the jealousy of the older child in relation to their siblings. It is something truly felt, I'm sure, but it also says a lot about the dynamic in many straight families. It implies that the father is at a net loss in this triangle. But they're not – they've also gained a child. And they've been promoted to a new role – dad.

We have here a dramatic schism that need not be so dramatic. But we also have a profound schism that is barely touched upon: the schism that opens up between the parents who have had a child and their friends who have not.


## Demotion

In my twenty years of childlessness, it is a break that I have often felt acutely. But one which I have felt both foolish and guilty about.

A friend or a friend's partner becomes pregnant. We celebrate with them, fantasise about the new life that we are going to welcome into our circle of friends. We talk about shared holidays, free babysitting, Uncle Ben and Uncle Tom.

We don't hear from our friends for a few days. A text comes. It is a picture of our friends more exhausted than we have ever seen them. The message reads 'Noah Linus, born midday. 7lb 3oz. Mother and baby doing well'.

We don't know how heavy 7lb 3oz is or whether that weight is good or bad.

In their arms in the photo is a tiny creature, skin scarlet-gold, the slit of one eye visible, a tuft of thin hair. Our friend is wearing what we assume are hospital clothes, she is sitting in a hospital bed surrounded by machines, by textures, colours and objects we know nothing about. The paraphernalia of childbirth, we divine.

We respond, but there is no reply. Our friends have entered a different world we cannot enter, in which priorities that had seemed so stable just a few days earlier have been turned on their heads.

A few more round-robin messages and emails arrive. We buy a present and after a week or two make an appearance with our gift of a onesie that we think is probably too big, because we couldn't understand the sizing.

'Thank you,' Mum says, holding up the onesie for Dad before looking around for a place to cast it off. You offer to take the onesie again. You hold it until you manage to find a surface to discreetly drop it on.

Your friends look different now. Their house smells different. They get out their breast in front of you and you don't know whether it's worse to swiftly look away or grin at their shockingly dark nipples.

You ask how the birth went and the story is told, but in vague terms. Contractions, a bath, a taxi. A bad midwife, a dismissive doctor, but then deliverance: a shift change and a good midwife.

You ask if you can hold the baby, but learn that this is no longer advised. The child needs to bond with the parents.

You do not volunteer anything about your own week and they don't ask you about it. What meaning would it have now? You tell them a story about your own birth, something that relates to what they've just told you, and they smile with sleepy beatification.

You go home and over the coming weeks and months you feel as if you have been demoted. And then you realise that you have been demoted. A new prince has been born. You have been shifted one place down the order of succession. You are removed one place from the affections of the monarch.

Your demotion is accompanied by a social promotion for the

new family. They are excused from all social obligations. They cancel lunches and dinners. When they do come, they arrive late and leave early.

Plans for shared holidays are cancelled. They mention a trip to Spain with new friends they made at their birth preparation class and when your face betrays your surprise they say, 'Oh, it's like a kids' resort. It'll be the worst. But it's the only way of doing it. You're well out of it.'

They increasingly respond to your disappointments by implying that they are deeply jealous of your life. 'God, I wish I was going on a work trip. A hotel room to myself – fuck. I would literally kill someone for it. Attack the breakfast buffet on my behalf. Please.'

But you know and they know that it's being a parent that matters.

Their joy is your loss. Your friends have gained a child, a family and all the status that that entails. But your life has become diminished. Worse, your loss is meaningless. It is indefensible. What hellish kind of egotist laments the birth of their friend's child?

Of course, sexuality and gender are working their magic here too. If this demotion is felt generally, it is complemented by a specific set of judgements for men and women, queer and straight. The childless straight man is seen as a mysterious, roguish figure. The childless queer man becomes a beloved uncle, the childless queer woman a beloved aunt – both seen as increasingly sexless, their emotional inner lives increasingly discounted until they are found at a party in tears by a nephew who is forced to confront the fact that they might have had the same dreams and the same disappointments as anyone else in the family.

Most pity is reserved for the childless straight woman. She tells us that she always felt deeply ambivalent about having children anyway.

'It's so crazy that it's even a topic of conversation these days,' we say.

But, of course, we don't believe her. Just as we smile supportively at the bisexual, believing they're on a journey to one side of the binary or the other, so too do we believe that the childless woman is making the best of a bad situation; that, deep down, if she was really honest with herself, she hoped things had been otherwise.

Even the woman who says she never wanted children is met with tight smiles and encouraging words. But in the taxi home, we turn to each other and say: 'Wait until she hits thirty-five. She'll come round.'

# 10

# Separation Pains

## The Fantasy of German Efficiency

'Have you got a nursery place yet?' our midwife asked us on her first visit, twenty-four hours after we had met our son. We shook our heads. When, a few weeks later, I called the nearest nursery to ask to go on their waiting list, the woman on the phone said, 'Has the child been born yet?' I had a sinking suspicion that we were already too late.

The free full-time childcare paid for by the Berlin government is a glorious luxury (which should, of course, not be a glorious luxury in a wealthy country). But the flipside of this great blessing is that competition is fierce for every nursery place and the application process is deeply disorganised and inefficient.

German efficiency is, it is worth saying, a myth. Or better put, it is a misreading of something more complicated. A misreading of Germans' belief in rightness; the fundamental belief that with enough thought and enough work a correct solution can be found for everything. And once that correct solution has been pinpointed, it necessarily should be applied in all contexts.

This approach often leads to things working very logically and thus efficiently. Your tap will always be a mixer tap because it works more efficiently than two separate taps and if your tap breaks you go to the DIY store and discover that every part of your tap is standardised and highly replaceable. Your tap is rather charmless, because it looks like everyone else's tap, but it does its job perfectly. You barely think about it from one year to the next.

But this belief in logic also leads to well-meaning bureaucratic processes that aim to be completely egalitarian but crumble in the face of human vagaries. And the nursery application system is a case in point. The (well-intentioned) belief in Berlin is that nursery places should be free, you should be able to choose which nursery suits you best and the application process for a nursery should be as simple as possible. You just pick one of the nurseries close by and call them to book your place. German rightness at its finest.

The practical reality that this set-up comes up against is that there aren't enough nurseries in Berlin and the relative number of children in different parts of the city shifts much more quickly than new nurseries can be opened to accommodate them. The 'fair' application process means that anyone can apply to any nursery. But this also means that it is common for determined parents to apply to thirty or more nurseries before their child is even born and then regularly phone round until they secure a place, knowing that the nursery directors have complete power to pick whichever parents they want to take.

What should be a simple system open to all becomes a system in which middle-class parents with all the right resources, chutzpah and language skills box their way into all of the best nurseries, leaving no places for the parents who follow the guidance and get in contact with the nursery a few months before their child should be joining.

We applied to eight nurseries a few months after Theo arrived. Only one offered us a place after a last-minute dropout. The relief, though, when we got the call was like hearing that he'd got into Yale.

## Never Let Me Go

Theo started going to nursery when he was two. In Berlin – partly because it's free, but partly because half the residents of the city grew up in East Germany, a state in which kids went to nursery after six weeks – this was considered pretty late. Most parents in our neighbourhood put their children into *Kita** the moment their fourteen months of parental leave were over.

'Where were you before?' parents kept asking me on our first day.

'Before what?'

'Which nursery were you in before this one?'

'Oh! No, we're just starting. He was at home with us until now.'

'Huh!' they would say, with a wide-eyed smile. I felt, for the first time in my life, like some sort of crazed hippy.

I was looking forward to Theo going to nursery. I think Tom would say that his main struggle with parenting is the relentlessness of parenthood and his anxieties around things that could happen to our son. While I share those challenges, my main day-to-day struggle is with boredom. I have always been very easily bored and I realise, as I get older, that I'm actually afraid of it. I am never without my headphones and a book, just in case there are a few seconds of the day in which I might be

---

* Inevitably, we don't actually call nursery 'kindergarten' in Berlin, but rather *Kita*, which is short for *Kindertagesstätte* ('child day place').

left with just my thoughts. Even if I'm hanging up the laundry or making myself lunch, I'll be listening to an audiobook or a podcast – music doesn't cut it. It's not distracting enough.

The trouble with parenting a small child is that it is extremely repetitive and involves huge stretches of time in which you cannot switch off, but in which you also cannot concentrate on anything else. So for me, the most challenging years were the crawling years.

The moment Theo was mobile and not just sleeping on my chest, I didn't want to have the TV on all day because he would've been watching it. But I also couldn't read a book; I had to keep a constant eye on him. So, for the best part of a year, I sat for hours on the largest rug we could find at Ikea watching him bash brightly coloured objects into the teal pile. The ambivalent joy of these years is best summed up by the fact that my two favourite moments of the day were when he woke up and when he fell back asleep again.

So the prospect of Theo being at nursery for seven hours seemed like bliss.

In summer, just before he went, I had wheeled him into a nearby Korean restaurant for lunch and asked a woman at a neighbouring table whether she minded me parking his buggy between her table and mine.

She looked up slowly, smiled behind her Sophia Loren-sized sunglasses. 'Oh, of course,' she said languidly, laying the novel she had been reading beside a bottle of beer beaded with condensation. 'I was in here with my pram a couple of months ago too. But now my son's in nursery.'

It was like meeting someone who'd found God. And for the next six months all I could think about was when I was going to get my moment at the corner table with a book and a cold beer. But, as is always the case, things turned out a little differently for me.

In Germany, nurseries use a three-week-long induction process called the 'Berlin Model', which involves going into nursery with your child for an hour a day, leaving them for ten minutes on the third day and then slowly adding on ten minutes each day until they are eating and napping at the nursery.

When I was first told about this approach, I thought it was sweet, but a bit over the top. I remember just being dropped off at primary school aged five and my mum being told she shouldn't wait outside otherwise I'd get too upset. I wailed so much that I had to be taken into the staff room to be told my crying was disturbing the other children. Didn't do me any harm, as the saying goes.

The first week of Theo's induction was filled with bad auguries. A giant rat crossed our path on the first day. On the second morning there was a thunderous summer shower, and when I went to get his buggy from the municipal bike shed in our building it was covered in shit. Sodden from running across the courtyard in the rain to get to the bike shed, I tried to wipe off as much faeces as I could using a mini pack of wet wipes. It was the dung of some nocturnal animal – a fox or a cat, I guessed – and it was everywhere.

Late now for our second morning, I made a temporary seat cover with a disposable changing-table cloth and pushed the buggy through the rain down the hill to the nursery. When we got home that afternoon, my neighbour revealed that someone had accidentally trapped a family of rats in the bike shed overnight – how they had gleaned this information, I cannot say – and they had gnawed and shat on everything.

Despite these inauspicious beginnings, the first days at the nursery went fine. It was August, the first summer of the Covid pandemic. I sat cross-legged on the orange carpet in shorts with Theo on my lap. The other children wandered over to show him battered toys, presented me with spoons from the toy kitchen for me to mime eating through my mask. After fifteen minutes, Theo got to his feet and gingerly walked over to a small wooden oven.

Halfway through the week I left him for the first time and was allowed to spend ten minutes in what our *Kita* glamorously refers to as the 'Parents' Café'. Because of Covid, the kettle and crockery had been removed, leaving just a pile of wooden toys and a set of books with worrying titles such as *When Your Partner Leaves*, *Divorce: The Best Answers to your Children's Questions* and *Marriage: A Challenge*.

I sat pensively on a red sofa with the novel I had optimistically brought with me shut on my lap. But when I punctually appeared again downstairs, Theo was playing with a wooden fire truck. He seemed cheerful and secure.

'He's doing very well,' his nursery teacher said, grinning. 'I think this is going to be a very smooth transition.'

As the minutes banished to the sofa turned into hours, I realised that I had been thinking about the nursery induction the wrong way round. While Theo seemed cautious but secure in those first weeks, I began to struggle. Another child bit him. Twice. The nursery teacher had seen the first bite, but not the second, which I discovered on the soft white skin of his upper arm when I was getting him ready for bed that night. A horrible bruise, two studded broken arches like the inside of a papaya that turned rust brown after a few days.

During the second week, I dropped him off and he ran into the adjoining room where the older children were. I wasn't sure if I was allowed to follow him, so I watched him go. Reflected in the glass in the door, I saw an older boy walk up to Theo and bend down to look into his face as he grabbed his ear and twisted it.

Theo didn't scream straight away; he didn't seem to understand what was happening. Siblingless and learning to walk in the same week as the first Covid lockdown – which meant we hadn't yet made it to a playground – he had been so sheltered up until the age of two that he had never even been shoved by another child. I strode into the room and barked at the older child and then barked at the nursery teacher, who ran through, white-faced, and apologised for leaving them unattended.

I felt like I'd failed Theo and I started to lose any sense of why we were bringing him to this institution in which, clearly, he was in danger.

But this wasn't even the moment that upset me most. The worst moment was when I went down to collect him a bit earlier than planned and I saw him at the little table eating his lunch with his big flannel bib on beside his little nursery friends. He was doing so well, being so brave all on his own without us, spooning yoghurt into his mouth surrounded by other children spooning yoghurt into theirs. It broke my heart.

Then Theo started to struggle. In the third week I was able to leave him on his own for ninety minutes, but he started to regress. One of the nursery staff would come and fetch me early saying he was too upset and I needed to come downstairs again. I would find Theo in his nursery teacher's arms, a lateral smear of teary snot across the man's olive green T-shirt.

'Theo needs to feel safe,' a mother told me outside *Kita*. 'You just need to believe he's going to be safe here and it'll all be fine.'

But I didn't believe he was going to be safe there. And I couldn't see how I ever would.

I knew that everyone who worked at the nursery was very competent and very nice. But it was a fact: they weren't going to care about his welfare as much as I or his Papa cared about it. Simple as that.

We plodded on, though. Every day, ten minutes before I was meant to go down to pick him up, someone would appear and tell me he was too upset. I had to come now.

I began to get pains in my joints. The doctor diagnosed me with 'mother's wrist' from lifting Theo out of his cot and I was given what seemed to me a rather Victorian electrotherapy that involved having wet flannels wrapped around the base of my hand and a pulsing current pumped through them.

The wrist got better, but I started getting pain in my ankles too, in my thighs. The doctor thought it could be arthritis, though it was odd, she admitted, that it was in my thighs. The pain would wake me up in the night, shooting up my legs, and from my wrists to my elbows. I was exhausted, but part of the 'Berlin Model' was that just one parent did the transition to nursery. Tom was not allowed to help.

Another week went by and we still couldn't get past ninety minutes of him at nursery without me. At the end of week seven I lay awake listening to Tom snoring, waiting for the ibuprofen to kick in so that I could fall asleep. I realised in the dark that we were going to have to take Theo out of nursery – it didn't make any sense. He was struggling, I was struggling. Nursery wasn't making my life any easier; it was the main source of my anxiety, in fact. I began to calculate how many years we could legally keep him at home before the government would make us send him to school. I wondered how difficult home-schooling really was.

The next day I came down from the Parents' Café to find Theo playing with another child. By the end of the week he had had his first nap at nursery and it was all over. He had been inducted.

My blood tests did not show any inflammation. My doctor suggested we wait until after Christmas to send me to a rheumatologist. A few months later the pain started to wane.

## The End of Adoption

Under German adoption law, you initially take in a child as an 'adoptive foster parent', which is followed by a year of house visits and then a court hearing which formalises the adoption. Generally, a mother who has had her child adopted is given a period of eight weeks in which she can change her mind. It is a sensible precaution, but the trouble for the adoptive parent is you cannot love a child conditionally.

During our adoption preparation course, we met a couple who now have two kids – one five, another just a few months old. But the first time they adopted, the mother changed her mind after week seven.

'The trouble is,' the adoptive mother said, her voice breaking, 'you take them home and you just love them. They're your baby.'

The loss of that first child had been so devastating that they had stopped the adoption search for a year. Six years later, they still struggled to talk about it.

So those sensible eight weeks feel like a lifetime for an adoptive parent.

Or at least they would if it really was eight weeks. In fact, for a range of reasons, emotional and practical, most mothers are unable to sign the papers at the end of the eight-week period. What ensues, until your court appointment, is a grey area in which you are regularly told by your social workers that it is very unlikely that there will be any issues with the adoption, but that they obviously can't make you any promises. So you have a year that feels like a lifetime.

Or at least it would if it really were a year. But, ironically, the more settled a child is and the better the placement is going, the less urgent the case is for the courts. And when, after eighteen months, you wonder if this week might be the week you get your court appointment, a global pandemic hits.

In the end we waited two years to adopt our son. Throughout that time we heard, countless times, 'It's going to be fine', 'I'm sure there's not going to be an issue', 'But what are the actual chances that something will go wrong?'

Those voices were right. But if I told you that your child was almost definitely not going to be taken away from you for the next two years, you would be terrified. And we were terrified. Every day we had to live with the possibility of profound loss.

After months of waiting for our court appointment I received a call from our social worker.

'The judge dealing with the case has asked for some more information before she makes a final decision. She has some last questions.'

I was not prepared for this. The judge bases their decision on a huge file that the adoption team at the Senate pull together over the adoption process and during the first years of the placement. It is filled with every conceivable detail about our upbringing, our health, our finances, our psychological, social and emotional suitability to become parents. And it ends with the social workers' recommendation that the child be adopted.

'OK,' I said. I hooked the phone under my ear and found a pen and a piece of paper. 'Fire away.'

'She would like to know what your coming out was like and whether you experienced any kind of social exclusion from your family or people more broadly.'

'Oh,' I said. 'That's odd. But fine. OK.' My pen hovered beside the next bullet point I had drawn, but there was silence at the other end of the phone. 'Anything else?'

'No, that was it. We'll do a new house visit and we can record your answers to the question for her.'

This one question led to a period of deep anxiety.

The fact that the adoption wasn't formalised was not only a psychological burden, it was also a practical frustration.

We had to register our son at nursery with a name that wasn't going to be the name he ended up with. He still had a court-appointed power of attorney who was his official legal guardian. They had to visit us every month. They had to write us a letter every time we visited my parents in England and agree in writing to any medical treatment our son was having.

But I was also frightened. At this point in the process, the judge's final agreement to the adoption was meant to be a rubber-stamping exercise. She had huge power over the decision to make our son's adoption legal, but the adoption team had done the work of preparing and making the recommendation. The judge should only be raising issues so serious that they might affect whether the child should be adopted or not.

I could see how, during the adoption process, our social workers might have been interested in hearing whether we had the support of our families or had experienced any issues around coming out. Indeed, part of the adoption process involved our social workers meeting members of our family, including our parents. But what was the judge hoping to find out that she couldn't already find in our thick adoption application?

Unlike our social workers, the judge deciding our case had no duty of care in relation to my husband and me. She did not tell our social worker why she wanted to know about our coming out. I was bothered by the fact that it was a question premised on a number of misunderstandings and judgements about being gay.

The first is that you have 'a coming out', but, as I mentioned in an earlier chapter, this is not the case. As a gay person, you often come out to friends and family over a long period of time and then you spend your life outing yourself every time you meet someone who doesn't know you.

There was also an assumption behind the question that

coming out could or should lead to marginalisation. Even if she did think such a question was relevant, she could have worded it without these assumptions. 'Have you ever felt socially marginalised in your life and, if so, do you think this might affect how you parent?'

That would have been better. But I still wouldn't have understood how this question might have affected the judge's final decision about whether we adopted or not.

When the social worker visited, our answer to the judge's question was: we didn't have a coming out in the way the question suggested we did. And we rarely felt marginalised, certainly not by our family, but the question did make us feel marginalised. It was a question that wouldn't have been asked of a straight couple and didn't seem to be relevant to the decision she was making in the light of the information she already had.

My best guess is that we were the first same-sex couple the judge had dealt with and that she was trying to come up with a question to reflect that. I don't know. We never met her.

Usually adoptees and their parents are invited to the hearing to decide on the child's adoption. Many of the gay parents I follow on Instagram post a photograph of this joyful moment at least once a year, their children dressed up smartly in tiny chinos, the judge grinning with them in front of the Queen's coat of arms or the American flag. But because of Covid, our social worker told us, a lot of the adoption hearings in Germany were taking place without the parents present. So we waited for the judge's response, not knowing if we were going to get an invitation to court or a confirmation that the hearing had already taken place without us.

So on a warm day in September, I arrived home from the supermarket with my son. I got him out of his buggy, got the shopping bag onto my shoulder and found, in our metal mailbox in the tiled hallway of our old block of flats – high and wide enough for carriages to pass through – a letter in a buff envelope. It was stamped with the address of the court.

I got Theo onto my hip and walked the four flights of stairs to our flat, my heart thumping. In our kitchen, I had time to read that the court hearing had taken place two days earlier and that, since that hearing, Theo had officially been our son. My eyes stung but I didn't have time to cry. Theo had managed to extract a half litre of strawberry yoghurt from the shopping bag and had emptied it into his lap. He was laughing as I carried him wriggling to the bath to wash it off, the letter stained and discarded by the kettle.

# Epilogue

What can differently formed families like ours tell us all about the essential assumptions we have about why we have children at all? We say we have children because we want to spread our genes. But what about us adopters and the non-biological parents of surrogate children? We say we have children because we are in love. But what about the single mothers inseminating themselves and raising their children alone? We say we have children because we want to live on in our kids. But what about the parents who give birth to and raise terminally ill children, knowing that they will outlive them?

People who hold up the straight nuclear family as an icon would have you believe that same-sex families are a danger to traditional families. But isn't there in fact something beautiful in the desire of people who can't biologically have children to have children anyway? Doesn't their desire not in fact undermine but rather reinforce the mysterious underpinnings of humans' desire for family?

Because, for all the difficulties, for all the financial, emotional and physical hardships involved in taking on children, there is something powerfully magical about becoming a parent. Same-sex parents, adoptive parents, single parents conceiving alone – these families show us that our desire to become parents is not just a matter of chemicals tricking fertile humans into mating and reproducing. These parents show us that most human beings, whatever their biological circumstances, have a deep, unerasable longing to subsume themselves in parental love. In this species infamous for its selfishness, there is in many of us an unquenchable yearning to put our every need below that of the children we love, to the point of oblivion if that's what it takes.

A century ago, celebrated scientists in the West were claiming that the explosion of free contraception would certainly lead to the extinction of the human race.[1] Who would have children if children weren't just a consequence of sex? Nontraditional families show us why we do.

I am someone who, once I had made sense of my sexuality as a teenager, grew up with no expectation that I would ever have a family. My emotional horizons were limited by the legislative landscape of the society around me. But the powerful effect of having a family when I thought I was never going to have one is that, every day, my son feels like a windfall.

Theo's adoption too gives me a powerful sense that, with the tiniest shift of circumstance – a party not attended, a move not made, a vote on gay marriage delayed – all of the joy of my family life would not exist. I see in my family the ways in which, in all of our lives, our happiness, like our sorrow, is held together for the briefest moment by time and happenstance.

When it comes to parenthood, both growing up gay and the experience of adoption teach you the same thing: that you and your children are never going to fit the image of the perfect family that has been sold to you since you were born. So you are free to abandon that image.

This realisation is painful. But as a queer person you are forced to deal with that realisation as a teenager. As an adoptive parent you are forced to deal with that realisation before you have even laid eyes on your child. This is your gift as a parent. You come to parenthood knowing that there is no perfect ending, no moment in which it's all going to be safe and sorted. You will always be in motion. Your joy, your security, your fulfilment will always be part of the churning wave of feeling, good and bad, that you will ride throughout your life until it breaks on some distant shore and disappears into the sand. This is, of course, true of all parents, though many only realise it after years of heartache.

Yesterday, a sunny day in mid-July, I picked up my son from nursery. I was tired and feeling guilty about collecting him a little bit too late and when I finally got there I discovered he had lost his sun hat.

I pushed his pram up the hill in the swampy Berlin summer heat – 30°C, but the humidity making it feel five degrees hotter. An unattractive line of sweat was already speckling my T-shirt beneath my chest and my belly.

Theo wanted ice cream. I tried to convince him that we should go to the supermarket where they sell the good ice cream, but he wanted one from the ice cream shop on the square we cross over on our way home. The ice cream isn't great there, but they have a giant fibre-glass ice cream outside the shop and will cover your scoops with a bucket of rainbow-coloured hundreds-and-thousands. It is thus irresistible to him.

We sat to eat our ice cream by the shallow fountain that the children like to paddle in. The heat in the previous weeks had covered the floor of the fountain with a slick of slippery algae and the surface had become greasy with sun cream. This did not deter the local children who slithered about perilously, naked or half naked in sodden, chocolate-stained T-shirts and vests, hobbled by soaked nappies.

Usually chatty in his Anglicised German, Theo ate in silence, frowning with concentration as he tried to stop the chocolate drips from running down his hands and the cone from collapsing into biscuity pieces. Two young men who had set themselves up in front of the outdoor tables of a nearby Lebanese restaurant began playing incongruous pop hits on the saxophone and guitar.

In the sticky heat of the afternoon, in the middle of a global pandemic, listening to the bad music, eating my bad ice cream, I watched my son's profile and thought: This is the moment that, on my death bed, I would swap all my worldly wealth to relive just one more time.

# Acknowledgements

This book is the result of a string of discussions with a number of generous and talented people. The idea for the book was sparked by an article I wrote for the *Guardian*, which I submitted after taking Ben Mauk's excellent pitching workshop in Berlin; I then discussed that pitch in detail with Hayley Camis at my publisher Little, Brown who was hugely enthusiastic about it and placed it with the *Guardian*. I am very grateful to her for that initial help and for her crucial support for this book when the proposal arrived at Little, Brown a few months later.

The idea of developing a book from the ideas discussed in the *Guardian* article came from my agent Karolina Sutton and I would like to thank her wholeheartedly for her work helping me put together the original proposal and for being so supportive of the resulting book. Her insightful notes and input have been completely invaluable. I would also like to thank both Caitlin Leydon and Joanna Lee at Curtis Brown for their ongoing help and support.

I would like to thank my editor Clare Smith at Little, Brown for seeing the potential in a kind of book very different from anything I've published before and without an obvious prototype already on the market. There is a lot of vocal discussion in the publishing world at the moment about supporting diverse voices but that talk rarely turns into publishers changing what they actually buy and how they sell it. What publishing needs more of is editors like Clare who have spent years quietly buying, publishing and believing in minority voices.

I am hugely appreciative of all the hard work the whole team at Little, Brown has put into this book, particularly Nico Taylor for his excellent jacket design, Nithya Rae for her efficient production work, and the editors Dan Balado and Rachel Cross for their eagle-eyed copyediting and proofreading.

This book has been hugely influenced by my reading the works of a number of brilliant writers, many of whom have been quoted in these pages. I owe a particular debt of gratitude, though, to Daniel Schreiber, who, as a writer, taught me how to merge the personal and the critical and who, as a friend, reminded me just to be honest whenever I got stuck telling this story.

The adoption process is necessarily an anonymous one and I am unable to mention by name all of the wonderful social workers in the Berlin Senate and in the Youth Welfare Offices in Berlin who guided us through our adoption. My gratitude towards them and the work they do under very difficult circumstances is, however, unending. They are genuine heroes.

I would like to thank my parents, Colin and Loraine, for giving me a very happy childhood and thus a foundation for how to parent. I saw time and time again in their parenting the ways in which they consciously handed down all the wonderful things they had experienced in their own childhoods, while trying to correct the things that had gone wrong. And I would like to thank both them and my parents-in-law, Hans-Peter and Gudrun, for being grade-A grandparents and calm voices of reason over these last few years.

As ever, I owe the biggest debt of gratitude to my husband, Tom. You have been the most constant support since the day I met you. I don't think I've ever met another person who has kept every promise they made to me. Having kids is tough but you have met it head on. You're a wonderful father and I'm so pleased I got to do all this with you.

But my biggest thanks has to go, of course, to my son Theo. You are a miracle. If I, as a father, can give you a tenth of what you give to me as a son every day then I'll be doing a pretty good job. I love you.

# Notes

## Chapter 1: Arrival

1   Ross, T. (2016), 'Boris Johnson: The EU Wants a Superstate, Just as Hitler Did', *Daily Telegraph*, 15 May.
2   Rhys, J. (2000), *Good Morning Midnight*, London: Penguin Classics, p.102.
3   Unsworth, E. J. (2019), '"I Lie to my Health Visitor. I Lie to Myself": The Truth about Postnatal Depression', *Guardian*, 8 June.

## Chapter 2: Fathoming a Family

1   Sedgwick, E. K. (1993), 'Queer Performativity: Henry James's The Art of the Novel', *GLQ: A Journal of Lesbian and Gay Studies*, 1(1), pp.1–16.
2   Lebowitz, F. (2021), *Pretend It's a City*, Netflix, Episode Two.
3   Ferrier, M. (2015), 'Domenico Dolce Apologises for Remarks about IVF and Gay Families', *Guardian*, 17 August.
4   Khan, C. (2021), '"I Miss the English Bants": Parminder Nagra on *ER*, *Bend It Like Beckham* and New Sci-Fi *Intergalactic*', *Guardian*, 14 April.
5   Sontag, S. (2009), 'On Camp', in *Against Interpretation and Other Essays*, London: Penguin Classics, p.275.
6   Staff, T. (2020), 'Education Minister Slammed for Suggesting Gay Marriage is Unnatural', *The Times of Israel*, 10 January.

7   Bawagan, J. (2019), *Scientists Explore the Evolution of Animal Homosexuality*, Imperial College London; available at https://www.imperial.ac.uk/news/190987/scientists-explore-evolution-animal-homosexuality/ (accessed 29 April 2021).

8   Nuwer, R. (2013), 'Same-Sex Parenting Can Be an Adaptive Advantage', *Smithsonian Magazine*, 27 November.

9   Mills, J. S. (1904), *Nature, The Utility of Religion and Theism*, London: Watts & Co., pp.9–10.

10  For an engaging history of same-sex sexual attraction, see Naphy, B. (2004), *Born to Be Gay: a History of Homosexuality*, Stroud: The History Press.

11  Rosenberger, J. G. et al. (2011), 'Sexual Behaviors and Situational Characteristics of Most Recent Male-Partnered Sexual Event among Gay and Bisexually Identified Men in the United States', *Journal of Sexual Medicine*, 8(11), pp.3040–50.

12  Hess, K. L. et al. (2016), 'Prevalence and Correlates of Heterosexual Anal Intercourse among Men and Women, 20 U.S. Cities', *AIDS and Behavior*, 20(12), pp.2966–75.

13  Hume, D. (1985), *A Treatise of Human Nature: Being an Attempt to Introduce the Experimental Method of Reasoning Into Moral Subjects and Dialogues Concerning Natural Religion* (ed. E. Mossner), London: Penguin Classics.

## Chapter 3: Hannah

1   BBC News (2018), 'In Search of Surrogates, Foreign Couples Descend on Ukraine', 13 February; available at https://www.bbc.com/news/world-europe-42845602 (accessed 14 December 2021). See also BBC News (2019), 'Surrogacy: Why the World Needs Rules for "Selling" Babies', 25 April; available at https://www.bbc.com/news/health-47826356 (accessed 15 December 2021).

2   Appiah, K. A. (2016), 'Is It Selfish for a Gay Couple to Have Kids via Surrogacy?', *New York Times*, 10 February.

3   Lewin, T. (2014), 'Coming to U.S. for Baby, and Womb to Carry It', *New York Times*, 5 July.

4   'About the Children' (no date), AdoptUSKids; available at https://www.adoptuskids.org:443/meet-the-children/children-in-foster-care/about-the-children (accessed 4 January 2022).

5   Catling, L. (2020), 'Germaine Greer Slams Elton John for Naming Husband as "Mother"', Mail Online; available at https://www.dailymail.co.uk/femail/article-8739313/Germaine-Greer-slams-Elton-John-naming-husband-mother-sons-birth-certificates.html (accessed 14 December 2021).

6   Zhang, S. (2021), 'The Children of Sperm Donors Want to Change the Rules of Conception', *The Atlantic*, 15 October.

7   This is based on a simple search of JSTOR for articles relating to 'ethics' and 'sperm donation' and then on 'ethics' and 'surrogacy'. The search was carried out on 4 January 2022.

8   Savabi-Esfahani, M. et al. (2019), 'Psychological and Social Consequences of Surrogacy in Surrogate Mother and the Resulted Child: A Review Study', *Iranian Journal of Obstetrics, Gynaecology and Infertility*, 22(4), pp.73–86.

9   Zhang, S. (2021), 'The Children of Sperm Donors Want to Change the Rules of Conception', *The Atlantic*, 15 October.

10  Nietzsche, F. W. and Large, D. (2007), *Ecce Homo: How to Become What You Are*, Oxford University Press (Oxford World's Classics), p.35.

## Chapter 4: Parent School

1   Mason, R. (2016), 'Priti Patel Warns of EU Migration Threat to UK Class Sizes', *Guardian*, 21 June.

2   Deutscher Bundestag – Grundgesetz für die Bundesrepublik Deutschland (no date); available at https://www.bundestag.de/gg (accessed 26 April 2021).

## Chapter 5: The Education Minister

1   *'Solange wir nicht wissen, ob es was verändert oder nicht, solange muss man diese Entscheidung doch nicht treffen.'*

2    And in fact research suggests that only 8 per cent of children of same-sex parents experience bullying related to having queer parents (see note 23). To put this in context, around 60 per cent of children experience some sort of bullying in school in the UK: Busby, E. (2019), 'Three in five children have been victims of bullying in school', *Independent*; available at https://www.independent.co.uk/news/education/education-news/three-five-children-have-been-bullied-school-survey-finds-a8995761.html (accessed 2 March 2020).

3    Mazrekaj, D., De Witte, K. and Cabus, S. (2020), 'School Outcomes of Children Raised by Same-Sex Parents: Evidence from Administrative Panel Data', *American Sociological Review*, 85(5), pp.830–56.

4    Rupp, M. (2009), 'Ergebnisse der ersten repräsentativen wissenschaftlichen Studie in Deutschland über Kinder in Regenbogenfamilien', Bundesjustizministeriums vom Bayrischen Staatsinstitut für Familienforschung an der Universität Bamberg.

5    Farr, R. H., Oakley, M. K. and Ollen, E. W. (2016), 'School Experiences of Young Children and their Lesbian and Gay Adoptive Parents', *Psychology of Sexual Orientation and Gender Diversity*, 3(4), pp.442–7.

6    Cody, P. A. et al. (2017), 'Youth Perspectives on Being Adopted from Foster Care by Lesbian and Gay Parents: Implications for Families and Adoption Professionals', *Adoption Quarterly*, 20(1), pp.98–118.

7    DK (2018), 'Studie: Kinder sind bei schwulen Vätern am besten aufgehoben', queer.de; available at https://www.queer.de/detail.php?article_id=31449 (accessed 28 November 2020).

8    Mazrekaj, D. et al. (2020), 'School Outcomes of Children Raised by Same-Sex Parents: Evidence from Administrative Panel Data', *American Sociological Review*, 85(5), pp.830–56.

9    McVeigh, T. and Finch, I. (2014), 'Fathers Spend Seven Times More with their Children than in the 1970s', *Observer*, 14 June.

10    Livingston, G. and Parker, K. (no date), '8 Facts about American Dads', Pew Research Center; available at https://www.

pewresearch.org/fact-tank/2019/06/12/fathers-day-facts/ (accessed 9 November 2021).

11 chance-quereinstieg.de, '6,6% Männer in Kitas' (no date); available at https://www.chance-quereinstieg.de/ aktuelles/detailansicht?tx_ttnews%5Btt_news%5D=1658&-cHash=1d193228e0d38d269911e5bb39bfd1f1 (accessed 9 December 2020).

12 Haug, K. (2017), 'OECD-Studie: Deutschlands Lehrer – älter, weiblich, gut bezahlt', *Der Spiegel*, 12 September.

13 chance-quereinstieg.de, '6,6% Manner in Kitas' (no date); available at https://www.chance-quereinstieg.de/aktuelles/ detailansicht?tx_ttnews%5Btt_news%5D=1658&-cHash= 1d193228e0d38d269911e5bb39bfd1f1 (accessed 9 December 2020).

14 Kaiser, T. (2019), 'Alleinerziehende Mütter: Ihre Zahl geht in Deutschland zurück', *Die Welt*, 14 July; Kramer, S. (2020), 'U.S. has world's highest rate of children living in single-parent households', Pew Research Center.

15 Boertien, D. and Bernardi, F. (2019), 'Same-Sex Parents and Children's School Progress: An Association That Disappeared Over Time', *Demography*, 56(2), pp.477–501.

16 Rudolph, K. (2020), 'Sieht Anja Karliczek ihren Irrtum über Regenbogenfamilien ein?', *Mannschaft Magazin*, 11 June.

17 This figure does not include the larger number of children adopted by step-parents or members of their extended families. 'Weniger Adoptionen in Deutschland, aber mehr Kinder von "Leihmüttern"', *Der Tagesspiegel*, 20 February 2018.

18 Bergold, P., Buschner, A. (2018), 'Regenbogenfamilien in Deutschland', bpb.de; available at https://www.bpb.de/ gesellschaft/gender/homosexualitaet/269064/regenbogenfam-ilien (accessed 18 December 2020).

19 'Mangel in vielen Bundesländern: Warum gibt es so wenige Pflegefamilien?', *Frankfurter Allgemeiner Zeitung*, 28 April 2019.

20 O'Hara, M. (2015), 'The LGBT Couples Adopting "Hard to Place" Children', *Guardian*.

21   Goldberg, A., Gartrell, N. and Gates, G. J. (2014), 'Research Report on LGB-Parent Families', UCLA Williams Institute; available at https://williamsinstitute.law.ucla.edu/publications/report-lgb-parent-families/ (accessed 18 December 2020).

22   'Great Britain: A Life of Concealment', *Time Magazine*, 27 September 1954.

23   Stotzer, R. L., Herman, J. L. and Hasenbush, A. (2014), 'Transgender Parenting: A Review of Existing Research', UCLA Williams Institute (preprint); available at https://escholarship.org/uc/item/3rp0v7qv (accessed 4 December 2021).

24   Murray, R. (2021), 'He Was Famous for Being "The Pregnant Man". Here's Where Thomas Beatie is Now', NBC News; available at https://www.nbcnews.com/nbc-out/out-community-voices/was-famous-pregnant-man-thomas-beatie-now-rcna1328 (accessed 4 December 2021).

25   Booth, R. (2020), 'Trans-Man Argues against Being Called Child's Mother at Appeal Court', *Guardian*, 4 March.

26   Goldberg, A. et al. (2014), 'Research Report on LGB-Parent Families', UCLA Williams Institute; available at https://williamsinstitute.law.ucla.edu/publications/report-lgb-parent-families/ (accessed 18 December 2020).

27   Morris, J. (2018), *Conundrum*, Faber & Faber, p.90.

28   Ibid., p.107.

29   Montreal Holocaust Museum (2019), Anti-Jewish Laws Timeline; available at https://museeholocauste.ca/app/uploads/2019/03/anti_jewish_laws_timeline.pdf (accessed 1 June 2021).

30   'German Jews during the Holocaust, 1939–1945' (no date); available at https://encyclopedia.ushmm.org/content/en/article/german-jews-during-the-holocaust (accessed 1 June 2021).

31   Levin, S. and Kamal, R. (2021), 'Mapping the Anti-Trans Laws Sweeping America: "A War on 100 Fronts"', *Guardian*, 14 June.

32   Devine, B. F. and Foley, N. (2020), 'Women and the Economy', House of Commons Library; available at https://

researchbriefings.files.parliament.uk/documents/SN06838/ SN06838.pdf (accessed 10 December 2020).

33   Hernandez, J. (2021), '1 in 4 American Jews say they experienced antisemitism in the last year', NPR, 26 October; available at https://www.npr.org/2021/10/26/1049288223/1-in-4-american-jews-say-they-experienced-antisemitism-in-the-last-year (accessed 8 November 2021).

34   Jonsson, U. (2017), 'Dame Julia Peyton-Jones is Selfish and Irresponsible to be a Mum at 64', *Sun*, 19 January.

35   '12 of Toni Morrison's Most Memorable Quotes', *New York Times*, 6 August 2019; available at https://www.nytimes. com/2019/08/06/books/toni-morrison-quotes.html (accessed 17 December 2020).

## Chapter 6: Closed Questions

1   UCLA Williams Institute (2018), 'How Many Same-Sex Couples in the US are Raising Children?'; available at https:// williamsinstitute.law.ucla.edu/publications/same-sex-parents-us/ (accessed 8 November 2021). This is based on an estimate of 50 million households in the USA with children under eighteen.

2   Bergold, P., Buschner, A. (2018), 'Regenbogenfamilien in Deutschland', bpb.de; available at https://www.bpb.de/ gesellschaft/gender/homosexualitaet/269064/regenbogenfam-ilien (accessed 18 December 2020). 'LGBT+ Parenting' (2021), FFLAG, 25 January; available at https://www.fflag.org.uk/ portfolio-item/lgbtplus-parenting/ (accessed 25 January 2021). When you realise that 0.0015 per cent of families being same-sex families in the UK is a global high, it does make you reflect on all those people arguing that same-sex marriage will lead to the destruction of the traditional family.

3   Solnit, R. (2017), *The Mother of All Questions*, Haymarket Books, p.5.

4   Romo, L. K., Dinsmore, D. R. and Watterson, T. C. (2016), '"Coming Out" as an Alcoholic: How Former Problem

Drinkers Negotiate Disclosure of their Non-Drinking Identity', *Health Communication*, 31(3), pp.336–45.

5   'Why Coming Out as a Conservative Is in No Way, Shape or Form "Almost Worse than Coming Out as Gay"', *PinkNews*, 2 December 2019.

6   Knor'malle, P. (2019), 'Coming Out as a Witch – Everything You Need to Know', *Medium*.

7   Eve Sedgwick (1990), *Epistemology of the Closet*, Berkeley, pp.3–4.

8   Lee, I. (2015), 'What I Discovered about Homophobia by Holding Hands with Another Man in Public', *Independent*, 12 January.

## Chapter 7: Consolations

1   King James Bible, Proverbs 3:5–6.

2   UNICEF Nutrition Section (2018), 'Breastfeeding: A Mother's Gift, for Every Child', United Nations Children's Fund.

3   The Nuffield Trust (2018), 'Breastfeeding'; available at https://www.nuffieldtrust.org.uk/resource/breastfeeding (accessed 29 April 2021).

4   Office for National Statistics (2019), 'Families and the Labour Market, UK'; available at https://www.ons.gov.uk/employmentandlabourmarket/peopleinwork/employmentandemployeetypes/articles/familiesandthelabourmarketengland/2019 (accessed 29 April 2021).

5   Livingston, G. and Parker, K. (no date), '8 Facts about American Dads', Pew Research Center; available at: https://www.pewresearch.org/fact-tank/2019/06/12/fathers-day-facts/ (accessed 9 November 2021).

6   Berical, M. (2019), 'What Nordic Dads Have That American Dads Don't', *Fatherly*; available at https://www.fatherly.com/love-money/swedish-dads-nordic-dads-survey/ (accessed 7 December 2021).

7   Burke, E. E. and Bribiescas, R. G. (2018), 'A Comparison of Testosterone and Cortisol Levels between Gay Fathers

and Non-Fathers: A Preliminary Investigation', *Physiology & Behavior*, 193, pp.69–81; 'Fathers' Brains Change When They Are the Primary Caregiver' (2014), *Independent*, 28 May.

8   Cusk, R. (2019), *A Life's Work*, Faber & Faber, p.103.

9   Mansfield, K. (2001), 'Bliss' in *The Collected Stories*, London: Penguin Books, p.93.

10  Johnson, A. (2014), *This Boy*, London: Corgi, p.32.

11  Young, M. and Willmott, P. (2013), *Family and Kinship in East London*, London: Routledge.

12  Reynolds, T. (2020), 'Studies of the Maternal: Black Mothering 10 Years On', *Studies in the Maternal*, 13(1).

13  Wax, E. (2004), '"In Africa We Carry our Children so They Feel Loved"', *Guardian*, 18 June. In many modern African nations a majority of mothers work. In countries like Nigeria, the labour force is in fact much more evenly split than in most Western nations, with business owners as likely to be female as male: PriceWaterhouseCooper (2020), 'Impact of Women on Nigeria's Economy', pwc.com, p.35.

14  Usman, B. A. (2017), 'Countries Where Women Are Most Active in the Workforce', WorldAtlas; available at https://www.worldatlas.com/articles/countries-where-women-are-most-active-in-the-workforce.html (accessed 5 January 2022).

15  Frizzel, N. (2018), 'You Can Smell a New Mother's Loneliness. Unless you're the State', *Guardian*, 3 May.

16  Plath, S. (2001), *The Bell Jar*, London: Faber & Faber, pp.61–2.

17  Office for National Statistics (2019), 'Families and the Labour Market, UK'; available at https://www.ons.gov.uk/employmentandlabourmarket/peopleinwork/employmentandemployeetypes/articles/familiesandthelabourmarketengland/2019 (accessed 15 June 2021).

18  Office for National Statistics (2019), 'Families and Households in the UK'; available at https://www.ons.gov.uk/peoplepopulationandcommunity/birthsdeathsandmarriages/families/bulletins/familiesandhouseholds/2019 (accessed 15 June 2021).

19  Harmanci, R. (2018), 'What No One Tells You About Not Being Able to Breastfeed', *The Cut*; available at https://

www.thecut.com/2018/05/the-truth-about-not-being-able-to-breastfeed.html (accessed 15 June 2021).

20   The original figure of 1 to 5 per cent was based on a 1985 study carried out at a time when breastfeeding was much rarer. Now that a majority of women in the US attempt to breastfeed, the figure has increased to 12 to 15 per cent. See Ibid.

21   'Official Laboratories Confirm Mineral Oil in Baby Milk' (2020), Foodwatch EN; available at https://www.foodwatch.org/en/news/2020/german-state-laboratories-find-mineral-oil-in-baby-milk/ (accessed 15 June 2021).

22   Krisch, J. A. (2018), 'The Hard Data Behind Why Dads Matter', *Fatherly*; available at https://www.fatherly.com/health-science/science-benefits-of-fatherhood-dads-father-effect/ (accessed 11 June 2021).

23   Caruso, R. (2019), 'The Science of How Fatherhood Transforms Men', *Today's Parent*, 8 June; available at https://www.todaysparent.com/family/parenting/the-science-of-how-fatherhood-transforms-you/ (accessed 15 June 2021).

## Chapter 8: Real Parents

1   Conn, P. (2013), *Adoption: A Brief Social and Cultural History*, New York: Palgrave Pivot, pp.26ff. The section that follows leans heavily on Conn's excellent history of adoption.

2   Ibid., p.27.

3   Ibid., pp.28ff.

4   King James Bible, Romans 8:15.

5   Conn, P. (2013), *Adoption: A Brief Social and Cultural History*, New York: Palgrave Pivot, pp.42–3.

6   Waters, S. (2002), *Fingersmith*, Virago.

7   Rossini, G. (2015), *History of Adoption in England and Wales*, Barnsley, South Yorkshire: Pen & Sword Books Ltd.

8   Wrobel, G. M., Helder, E. and Marr, E. (2020), *The Routledge Handbook of Adoption*, Milton: Taylor & Francis Group, p.3.

9   Rossini, G. (2015), *History of Adoption in England and Wales*, Barnsley, South Yorkshire: Pen & Sword Books Ltd, pp.54–64.

10  Wrobel, G. M. et al. (2020), *The Routledge Handbook of Adoption*, Milton: Taylor & Francis Group, pp.3–4.

11  Rossini (2015), *History of Adoption in England and Wales*, Barnsley, South Yorkshire: Pen & Sword Books Ltd, pp.95ff.

12  Murnane, J. (1999), 'An Inquiry into Adoption Rates in Ireland', *Econometrics: Theory and Practice*; available at https://www.tcd.ie/Economics/assets/pdf/SER/1999/John_ Murnane.pdf (accessed 12 November 2021).

13  Wrobel, G. M. et al. (2020), *The Routledge Handbook of Adoption*, Milton: Taylor & Francis Group, pp.4–5.

14  Winterson, J. (2012), *Why Be Happy When You Could Be Normal?*, London: Vintage, p.182.

15  Herman, E. (2012), *Adoption History: Adoption Statistics*, University of Oregon Adoption History Project; available at https://pages.uoregon.edu/adoption/topics/adoptionstatistics. htm (accessed 12 November 2021).

16  Rossini (2015), *History of Adoption in England and Wales*, Barnsley, South Yorkshire: Pen & Sword Books Ltd, pp.152–3.

17  Kynaston, D. (2010), *Family Britain, 1951–1957*, London: Bloomsbury, p.565.

18  US Department of State (2019), 'Adoption Statistics', travel. state.gov; available at https://travel.state.gov/content/travel/ en/Intercountry-Adoption/adopt_ref/adoption-statistics-esri. html?wcmmode=disabled (accessed 17 June 2021).

19  Fenton, E. (2019), *The End of International Adoption? An Unraveling Reproductive Market and the Politics of Healthy Babies*, New Brunswick, New Jersey: Rutgers University Press, p.14.

20  Ibid., p.3.

21  Walton, J. (2019), *Korean Adoptees and Transnational Adoption: Embodiment and Emotion*, London, New York: Routledge, p.4.

22  US Department of State (2019), 'Adoption Statistics', travel. state.gov; available at https://travel.state.gov/content/travel/ en/Intercountry-Adoption/adopt_ref/adoption-statistics-esri. html?wcmmode=disabled (accessed 17 June 2021).

23  Adoption Network (2020), 'US Adoption Statistics'; available at

https://adoptionnetwork.com/adoption-myths-facts/domestic-us-statistics/ (accessed 12 November 2021).

24  Adoption UK (2020), 'Adoption Rate Down by Third Since 2015'; available at https://www.adoptionuk.org/news/adoption-rate-down-by-third-since-2015 (accessed 16 June 2021).

25  Walton, J. (2019), *Korean Adoptees and Transnational Adoption: Embodiment and Emotion*, London, New York: Routledge, p.68.

26  Salesses, M. (2012), 'My Korean American Story: Matthew Salesses'; available at http://koreanamericanstory.org/written/my-koreanamericanstory-matthew-salesses/ (accessed 30 May 2021).

27  Verrier, N. (2009), *The Primal Wound: Understanding the Adopted Child*, London: British Association for Adoption and Fostering, pp.13–21.

28  Chalabi, M. (2013), 'Dads that Don't Live with their Children: How Many Stay in Touch?', *Guardian*, 20 November.

29  Rutherford, N. (2019), 'The Truth about Family Estrangement', bbc.com; available at https://www.bbc.com/future/article/20190328-family-estrangement-causes (last visited 4 March 2021).

30  Fenton, E. (2019), *The End of International Adoption? An Unraveling Reproductive Market and the Politics of Healthy Babies*, New Brunswick, New Jersey: Rutgers University Press.

31  Cancio-Bello, M. C. (2020), 'This Graphic Memoir About Adoption Isn't Interested in Comfortable Answers', Electric Literature; available at https://electricliterature.com/this-graphic-memoir-about-adoption-isnt-interested-in-comfortable-answers/ (last visited 4 March 2021).

32  Salesses, M. (2012), 'My Korean American Story: Matthew Salesses'; available at http://koreanamericanstory.org/written/my-koreanamericanstory-matthew-salesses/ (accessed 30 May 2021).

## Chapter 9: Childlessness

1   Stein, G., 'Man, Dying' in Gresko, B. (2014), *When I First Held You: 22 Critically Acclaimed Writers Talk About the Triumphs, Challenges, and Transformative Experience of Fatherhood*, New York: Berkley.

2   Margolin, E. (2014), 'Texas GOP Warns Gay Marriage Could Lead to Incest, Pedophilia', MSNBC.com; available at https://www.msnbc.com/msnbc/texas-gop-warns-gay-marriage-could-lead-incest-pedophilia-msna385616 (accessed 16 July 2021).

3   Chatel, A. (2016), 'These Were the Most Popular Porn Searches in the U.S. in 2015', Bustle; available at https://www.bustle.com/articles/133897-these-were-the-most-popular-porn-searches-in-the-us-in-2015 (accessed 16 July 2021).

4   Maxwell, W. (2001), *They Came Like Swallows*, London: Vintage, p.118.

## Epilogue

1   Holmes, S. J. (1932), 'Will Birth Control Lead to Extinction?', *Scientific Monthly*, 34(3), pp.247–51.